Florian Afflerbach

Freehand
Drawing

Florian Afflerbach

Freehand
Drawing

BIRKHÄUSER
BASEL

Contents

Foreword

For architects, depicting their own work is a most important means of presenting themselves to clients and the specialist world. In this context, the quality of a brief explanatory sketch or freehand drawing acquires particular importance, as they are often the only medium through which the work can be explained to outsiders. Freehand drawings are, additionally, an important planning tool that accompanies architects during the discovery of the idea and in the later planning and concretisation processes.

Depicting a building by means of freehand drawings makes a number of demands on the draughtsman or woman and naturally requires practice, but this skill can be acquired systematically – for instance by constructing perspectives. Knowledge about materials, aids and techniques help the person making the drawing to appropriate existing buildings and to understand their specific qualities better. These abilities are essential to be able to examine and communicate design ideas. It is precisely the subjective approach involved in freehand drawing that enables one to order one's thoughts and to concentrate on the important design approaches.

The volume *Freehand Drawing* forms an important element within the topic of *Fundamentals of Presentation.* To enable students to produce architectural drawings of a high quality, first of all the technical tools such as pens and drawing substrates are explained. The chapter "Freehand drawing in architectural design" describes different types of drawing and specific approaches to design. In the chapter "Architectural drawing on site" these themes are broadened to cover the area of drawing existing buildings. As the further development of drawings is part of daily life, different possibilities in this area and with regard to processing images are explained. Here, architecture students and other interested persons are given a broad and practical basis for producing their own freehand drawings of real quality.

Bert Bielefeld, Editor

Basic principles of freehand drawing

DISTINCTIONS AND TERMS

The theory of art defines sketches and drawings as part of the graphic arts. The instruments used for drawing (pencil, pastels etc.) are abraded as they are drawn across a substrate, generally paper, or form a liquid film (ink, watercolours etc.). The most obvious difference from painting is that lines are dominant rather than areas of colours. Consequently, sketches and drawings remain just a composition of lines, not colours and are therefore never paintings. What the hand, using the drawing instrument, puts on paper are the primary means of a drawing: point, line and surface. Sketches and drawings can be given greater expressive power by using complementary means such as spatial staggering in depth, colour, or the depiction of light and shade.

Freehand drawing is the basis for many kinds of artistic work: painting, sculpture and also architecture. It includes the sketch, a rapidly produced drawing in which depicting the typical characteristic is often more important than reproducing individual qualities and which, even more so than the drawing, aims at achieving a maximum of expression and power

Fig. 1: The Tagblatt Tower in Stuttgart, drawn using four different techniques (clockwise from top left): pencil with watercolours, pencil, chalk on brown paper, charcoal

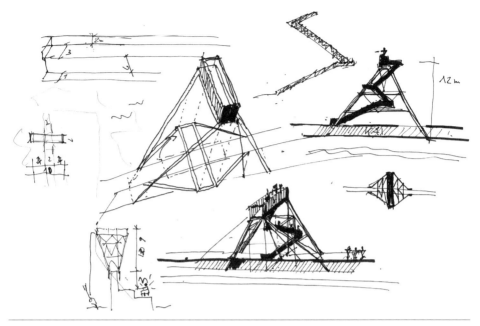

Fig. 2: Spontaneous sketches of ideas on a paper napkin (Antalya observation tower)

with little expenditure of technique and material. The <u>drawing</u> therefore always offers more information than the sketch.

Freehand sketching and drawing is generally used during the early stages of an architectural design, to depict ideas or concepts or to clarify basic questions about the form, construction or urban situation of a building. Sketches and drawings made at this phase can provide the basis for architectural models or technical drawings, which then make the design more concrete. They can also be made with rulers and stencils, if they have a design character. The boundary to technical drawing is blurred. The sketch can also be used in the later phases of a project, for example to show a detail for the detail design stage, > Fig. 54, page 53 or to provide instructions for skilled tradesmen working on the building site.

If architecture is drawn on site, the sketch is not based on imagination but is the depiction of a concrete reality based on looking directly at the building. > Fig. 3

Sketches and drawings are always a highly individual mirror as the skilled hand, raw force and tenacious impatience can be read from them,

Fig. 3: Architectural sketch made on site (Fundação Iberê Camargo, Alvaro Siza, Porto Alegre)

telling us much about how they were made and the particular nature of the <u>author</u>. In contrast to photography they are made gradually and thus interact with the person who produces them, who is in permanent visual contact with what he or she has already put on paper.

Drawing and sketching in architectural design or drawing architecture on site is determined by a selective way of working. Certain things are omitted so that they do not distract, or important aspects are emphasised so as to depict them in a focused way. It can therefore be said that the expressive content of the empty, untouched areas of a drawing is equal to that of the treated areas. This moment of imprecision further distinguishes the drawing from photography, which generally records everything within the viewing angle of the lens, or from the CAD drawing, which often includes unnecessary information. > Fig. 80, page 77: the brain can imagine the appearance of the annexes as they have similar building forms.

DESIGN MEDIUM

Freehand sketching is an elementary part of all design phases that call for design, functional or construction-related decisions. It functions as intellectual <u>preparatory work</u>, which is repeatedly rejected and renewed until the pure drawing of the final version is produced using the methods of technical drawing.

The combination of a roll of sketching paper and pencil, a place to build models and the CAD program is the ideal workplace for the designing architect. Freehand drawing is particularly useful for spontaneous and creative work, as ideas can be put down directly on paper with minimal interruption to the flow of thought.

The early sketch made during the design stage, still unaffected by any kind of political, financial or constructional pressure, is the moment when the architect's idea appears in its pure and unadulterated form. This spontaneity and intuition underline the subjective nature of the freehand drawing which, as it is made by hand, is directly connected to the author and thus to the architect's drawing language.

The increased use of CAD programs in the early design stages makes drawing styles seem more uniform and interchangeable. Designers subject themselves to the rules of the CAD system in terms of graphics, scale and norms, although the sketch is in fact graphically independent, without scale and non-binding. A gap that apparently can no longer be closed is opening up between the architect's understanding and his hand, as something that is virtual – the design – is also being produced virtually.

Later design phases, too, throw up problems that call for new ideas, variations and improvements. Freehand sketching and drawing can also use a greater degree of detail and a different scale to arrive at solutions and can therefore accompany a project right up to its <u>completion</u>. > Chapter Freehand drawing in architectural design, Continuing the design

INSTRUMENT OF COMMUNICATION
The architect must be able to communicate his or her ideas and concepts in a way that can be correctly read and understood by the viewer. While still a student, teachers and fellow students are the main recipients for these ideas, whereas in professional life it is colleagues, clients, tradespeople, public authorities or the general public to whom certain contents must be conveyed quickly and directly.

The drawing is the <u>language</u> of the architect. As part of the design process sketches are made all the time during brainstorming sessions, and on the building site sketches are used daily in discussions with construction workers. If the descriptive perspective drawing, legible by a lay public, that is frequently called for in architecture competitions is drawn freehand this has the advantage that, unlike finely detailed, photorealistic computer renderings, it does not yet have a final character and does not lay down a detailed architectural direction. Here it is not decisive whether a perspective drawing is made with the help of technical drawing

Fig. 4: Hand-drawn perspective for a competition

instruments (ruler, compass, parallel straightedge or similar) or is drawn freehand. The important aspect is the unfinished and incomplete quality of the drawing, which leaves leeway for the imagination of viewers who may have little understanding of architecture. The drawing becomes an intermediary. > Fig. 89 below, page 86

PERCEPTION

Drawing buildings directly on site offers an excellent opportunity to understand architecture better. The permanent interplay between direct observation and the drawing being created allows the structures, proportions and other formative aspects that describe the building to be grasped precisely. What is seen and then drawn imprints itself on the memory. The information gained in this way can be used for comparative purposes in the next on-site architectural drawing, or in a future design project. Architectural drawing on site does not mean simply the depiction of what is seen but the reflective processing of form, function or construction.

The drawing is a collection of transported and interpreted impressions that have made their way onto paper. The lines, colours and hatch-

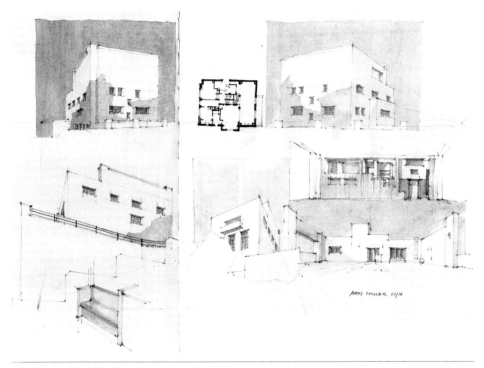

Fig. 5: Visit to the Müller House (Adolf Loos, Prague)

ing are metaphors for what has been perceived. In recognising what was drawn the viewer converts these metaphors back into reality. The drawing is therefore not simply a tool for depicting but also (for both draughtsperson and viewer) an <u>intellectual tool</u>. The drawing illustrates what has been considered and records what has been perceived. In precisely observing the subject, the person drawing it is confronted with new questions.

The city provides excellent opportunities for the architectural draughtsperson who wishes to draw on site, through the abstract aspect of the drawing it is broken down from three to two dimensions. Perspective drawing in the city includes making use of certain rules and guidelines in order to depict the architecture correctly and with a high level of content. By adding people, vegetation, cars, data and atmospheric impressions, snapshots are made that illustrate experiences of time and space. Yet the architectural drawing can never replace actually making a visit to a building.

Tools and techniques

DRAWING SUBSTRATES

Drawing boards, drawing tables and T-squares have become so rare in the professional life of the architect today that large sheets or rolls of paper are practically never used. CAD programs with an infinitely larger user interface and plotters that transfer the drawing to paper take over the large-scale work. Consequently, the selection below is restricted to drawing substrates in the form of smaller sheets of paper.

First of all we should focus on those substrates that can be considered for the design process. Essentially, every kind of paper substrate can be used as the basis for a freehand drawing – including scraps of paper, notes or even beer mats or paper napkins.

Sketchbooks are valuable companions both during the design process and for the architectural drawing on site. Information, ideas, architecture sketches and interesting things from everyday life can be recorded in them permanently and developments documented.

Working with the sketching paper roll

The most important kind of paper in the design process is the sketching paper roll. This is very thin, transparent paper rolled around a cylindrical cardboard core. The sketching paper roll is generally around 30 cm wide and has a length of between 20 and 100 m. It is available in different paper strengths from 20 to 40 g/m² of wood-free cellulose, the thicker papers (unit: g/m²) being less translucent. It is generally transparent-white; brownish or corn yellow sketching paper rolls are rarer. They offer the advantage that white pencils or chalks can be used on them to emphasise certain lines and surfaces.

The sketching paper roll can be used in every design phase whenever ideas and studies must be given a sketched visual form and different versions and examinations are necessary. It offers a number of advantages.

Sketching paper rolls are relatively inexpensive. This aids the creative flow, as there are no financial repercussions if a sketch just made has to be torn off the roll, crumpled up and tossed into the waste-paper basket. This paper is there to be thrown away, as in this phase sheets from rolls of sketching paper are the bearers of a wealth of good and bad ideas that are examined on the next piece of paper from the long roll. In this way the design gradually grows more concrete.

Fig. 6: Roll of sketching paper with a design sketch laid over as-built drawing

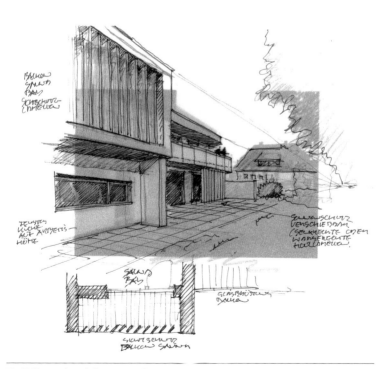

Fig. 7: Illustration of changes to a building: roll of sketching paper over a photograph

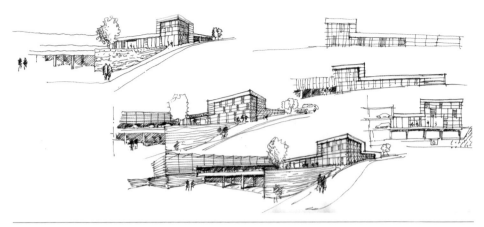

Fig. 8: Alternatives, produced with the roll of sketching paper

To produce different versions and variations and to examine their contents, the roll of sketching paper is laid over an existing drawing. Here it does not matter whether this is one's own drawing, a drawing by a colleague, as-built plans from a current project, or plans made with the computer. The roll of sketching paper can be laid over every kind of drawing – and even across the computer screen.

Changes or improvements are repeatedly drawn on new translucent layers of paper. The paper's translucency makes direct comparison with the earlier sketch possible. This procedure can be repeated until the desired goal is achieved.

But the sketching paper roll can also be used as drawing substrate without any other drawing beneath it. In particularly tall or long buildings, situations can arise where a long piece of paper is needed in order to draw an elevation, a section or a certain perspective.

In drawing perspective by the intersection point method the sketching paper roll can also be used. > Chapter Freehand drawing in architectural design, Drawing types The drawings needed for this method (elevation and plan) are placed beneath the translucent paper and fixed in position. This allows the perspective to be made on its own sheet of paper, separated from the elevation and plan. > Fig. 64, page 60

Tracing paper

If the paper in the sketch roll is found to be too thin or not sufficiently resistant, another kind of paper combines the quality of the sketching paper roll with that of normal paper: tracing paper. It is thicker than sketching paper (80 to 200 g/m²) and consequently less transparent, which can lead to the problem that the drawing beneath is not completely legible.

Tracing paper generally comes in sheets in DIN A formats and also, but more rarely, in rolls. Compared to the sketching paper roll, tracing paper is more suitable for drawing instruments with hard tips such as ballpoint pens and classic ink pens with different line widths. Incorrect lines can be scratched away using a razor blade or special kinds of erasers. However, this also removes the uppermost layer of the tracing paper and care must be taken to avoid scratching a hole in the paper.

Drawing paper

The most undemanding paper for freehand drawing is simple, brilliant white, wood-free drawing paper or <u>drawing card</u>, which resembles multi-function printer paper. It has the character of an empty sheet of paper and at the start of a project represents in a metaphorical sense a "tabula rasa" for free drawing without any influences.

It is available in different thicknesses from 80 to 300 g/m² and generally in DIN A formats. It is not ideally suited to any specific drawing instrument. > Tab. 1 This kind of paper is more an "all-rounder". Lines drawn on it with water- or alcohol-based pens bleed easily. If they are too watery, watercolours cause the paper to tear or to become wavy. Hard tips, such as ballpoint pens and hard pencil leads, often print through the paper and, if a pad or block is being used, leave a relief-like imprint on the next page. Lined paper is not really suitable for sketching. If a design is being drawn at a particular scale, squared paper provides beginners with a sure guide as regards dimensions.   ○

Grey and brown paper

Compared to white papers, of which there is a wide range, greyish and brownish paper offer the advantage that white lines and areas can be draw on them, and the brightest part of the drawing does not have to be paper untouched by the drawing, as is the case with white paper.

○ **Note:** The rule of thumb is: the finer the grain, the thinner the paper, and the smoother the surface of the paper the more suitable it is for hard drawing instruments such as pencils or ink and felt pens. Markers can also be used more easily on smooth paper, as the lines and areas of colour do not bleed to such an extent. Conversely, coarse-grained paper is better for watercolours, soft pencils or charcoal and pastels. It should be acid-free as this means it is resistant to ageing and can also be used for inks and watercolours.

Fig. 9: Heights and depths using white and black on brown paper

Fig. 10: Heights and depths with white and black on yellow paper

This is ideal for emphasising areas or surfaces, space and atmosphere. For instance: in a perspective, colouring the sides of the building that stand in the sun white and those in the shade black makes the line drawing more spatial and atmospheric. It is also easier to indicate differences in the materials used in the planned buildings. The grey or brown area of the paper that remains untouched by lines and blocks of colour
■   then stand for a middle tonal value that is in neither sun nor shade. > Fig. 9

Sketchbooks

The prospective architect should keep a sketchbook in which the progress of a design can be documented and which offers the opportunity to note down an idea, something seen or a piece of information. Sketchbooks are available in wide variety of shapes and sizes, but for an architect's purposes some kinds are more suitable.

A freehand sketch or drawing is generally not to scale and therefore is as large as you draw it. Nevertheless, the <u>size</u> of the sketchbook page should be at least DIN A5 in horizontal or upright format. A large drawing surface offers the advantage that, for example, the vanishing points of a perspective frequently still lie on the sheet, or there is room enough for a further idea on the same sheet. Therefore small sketchpads and ring books with individual pages are unsuitable. If you need to make a smaller drawing you can drawn a small frame or outline on the existing sheet.

Tab. 1: Combinations of different drawing grounds and drawing instruments (++ very good, + good, o middling, - bad, – very bad)

	Sketching paper roll	Tracing paper	Drawing paper	Multifunction paper up to 120 g/m²	Multifunction paper from 120 g/m²	Grey and brown paper	Watercolour paper	Marker paper
Hard pencil	-	++	o	+	+	o	o	-
Soft pencil	++	+	+	o	++	++	+	-
Coloured pencil	+	+	+	o	+	o	o	—
Felt pen	++	+	o	+	o	+	-	o
Ink pen	++	++	+	+	+	+	-	+
Ballpoint pen	—	-	+	o	o	o	—	o
Pastels and charcoal	-	—	o	o	++	++	+	-
Markers	++	+	-	-	-	—	-	++
Watercolours	—	—	+	o	+	—	++	o

Sketchbooks need to be filled. Drawing by drawing a fine collection can be built up, a travel sketchbook, or the chronology of one's own progress. Sketchbooks accompany their owner over a longer period of time and should therefore have a sturdy cover with thread-stitched pages. This kind of cover also can serve as a base or support when drawing. The paper should be acid-free and have a thickness of at least 150 g/m². The kind of paper depends entirely on the drawing instrument chosen. If you use mainly pencil and watercolours, you should choose coarse-grain or even watercolour paper. For markers and ballpoint pens smooth paper is more suitable. > Tab. 1 ∎

■ **Tip:** This technique can also be used with sketching paper or tracing paper. If using tracing paper the white is applied to the back to avoid contact with the pencil or ink lines drawn on the front. This also has the advantage that the area to be covered in white can be drawn more clearly.

■ **Tip:** Some sketchbooks have useful features that improve everyday (sketching) life. Some have an attachment to hold the pencil, other have a pocket inside the back cover to take visiting cards or similar information. With smaller sketchbooks an external rubberised band is an advantage, as it prevents the book from opening accidentally when in a bag or satchel. Sketchbooks with rounded corners prevent dog-ears.

Fig. 11: Sketchbooks of different sizes and with different kinds of paper, some with a bookmark or rubber band

Keeping a sketchbook

Everything that interests an architect can be kept in a sketchbook: from sketched ideas about town planning to a window detail, written notes and illegible doodles made during a talk given by a colleague, architectural drawings made during travels, everyday situations and objects of all kinds that are sufficiently interesting to make a drawing worthwhile.

In drawings with an informative or even narrative character, <u>writing</u> can be a meaningful addition. Some things are best understood in a drawing, others are better written down: assessments about a material, smells, descriptions of a colour for making a wash later, names (or even personal signatures) of people you have to deal with in a project, or references to certain impending or past events which you wanted to note quickly.

If a sketchbook is used <u>chronologically,</u> it can develop into a kind of personal life story with the character of a diary that you can use as an encyclopaedic store of knowledge for future design projects. Known as journaling, this aspect is illustrated by the constantly growing range of notebooks now available that cater for different professions, places or personal interests.

Fig. 12: Open sketchbooks with notes, design sketches and on-site drawings

Keeping a sketchbook also forms a counterpart to digital photography, which makes it possible to take large numbers of pictures everywhere and at all times. Sketchbooks you have filled yourself are full of your own observations and through the author's <u>subjectivity</u> they acquire a pure form of individual identity. You can also record you own memories in them. On looking later at sketches you have made, you recall the subjects and being reminded of them again may even mean that they are stored in your long-term memory.

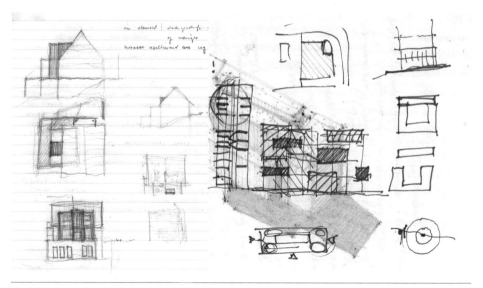

Fig. 13: Somewhat illegible, intimate design sketches

LINES AND THE INSTRUMENTS FOR DRAWING THEM
Lines

Like the technical drawing, a freehand drawing also consists largely of lines that vary in terms of form and weight from drawing to drawing. They can be used to depict almost everything in drawing and sketching architecture: from site boundaries, building outlines and edges to individual storeys and to wall constructions, furniture and door handles. But it is only through accentuation, different kinds of lines and the differentiated use of strokes in different sizes and scales of drawings that the sketch becomes legible and understandable. Sketches illegible to outside observers are intended only for the author and help transfer important information to the next design stage. > Fig. 13

The lines that gradually create the design grow more concrete over the course of time to form a sketch or drawing. Here the draughtsman or woman constantly improves what has been drawn, rejects it, erases it or – in the best case scenario – finds it good. The draughtsperson always sees what has been "done" a moment previously, engaging in an emotional relationship with what has been drawn. Object – eye – hand – pencil – paper: a complex sequence of activities and reactions is concealed behind creative drawing.

In on-site architectural drawing the dimension of this interaction changes: you do not compare what has been drawn with the image in

Fig. 14: On-site architectural drawing, where edges, changes of material, colour and light (here shown as dotted lines) are abstracted and depicted as strokes.

your head but with the depiction of real architecture. We do not draw imaginary lines but rather we abstract outlines that do not exist in real nature. > Fig. 14 We interpret them as lines, although in fact only a change of volume, material, colour or light takes place. We therefore draw the visual <u>boundary</u> between two volumes (or material or colours), a boundary between light and shade or between a volume and the air surrounding it as a line.

○

Types of lines

Although freehand drawing and sketching tends to be a relatively fast activity and must not comply with the rules of technical drawing, it nevertheless makes sense to differentiate between the most common types of lines: full lines, dashed or broken lines, and dotted lines. Differences cannot be made between <u>line thicknesses</u>, as in each sketch this depends on the instrument with which the lines are drawn. Nevertheless, sketches that use a wide variety of different line thicknesses are more vivid and more legible.

○ **Note:** The dot-dash line familiar from technical drawing is not commonly used in freehand drawing, as it denotes axes and section lines, which are generally not considered in the early design stages.

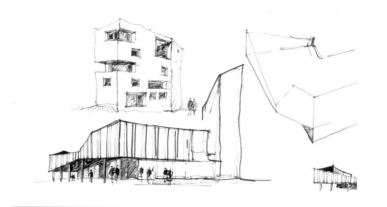

Fig. 15: Sketch elevation made with different line thicknesses; the volume at the bottom left is emphasised by the use thicker outlines.

Full lines are those used to describe all the visible edges of objects and building parts in a depiction. In section drawings the parts of the buildings cut through are indicated by the use of thicker lines. In elevations the line of the ground is emphasised. Buildings in the foreground are often given heavier outlines and shown with thicker lines than the less important edges or parts of the building in the background. > Fig. 25, page 31

Broken lines (also known as dashed lines) denote volumes, building parts, or other important edges that lie behind or beneath the actual depiction. Dotted lines, on the other hand, describe the edges of building parts that are over or above what is depicted. Dotted lines should truly consist of dots. The need to use dashed or dotted lines in depicting building parts arises particularly frequently in floor plans or section drawings.
> Chapter Architectural drawing on site, Drawing types

Drawing correctly

Straight lines should be drawn straight. Frequent mistakes include lines that, due to the given radius between wrist and arm, are drawn curved although in fact they should be straight. Care should also be taken that a line consists of only a single line. To draw straight ground lines the little finger can be led along the edge of the table or of the sketchbook at the same time drawing a straight line parallel to this edge. A second line should not be drawn over an interrupted or broken line in order to correct it. The interrupted line can be continued at a slight distance. > Fig. 16

Lines that represent building corners, for example, should always consist of two intersecting lines. The lines of a volume that lie behind

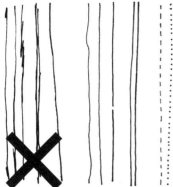
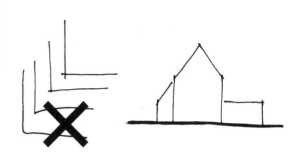

Fig. 16: Incorrectly and correctly drawn lines, full lines, dashed lines and dotted lines

Fig. 17: Correct and incorrect corners, the lines of the building volumes in the background are separated somewhat from the main volume.

another volume should not cut its lines and should be drawn somewhat separated.

Hatching

Hatching allows us to create surfaces, shadows or to indicate materials with the use of lines. It should not be confused with the different kinds of hatching used to denote specific materials in technical drawings. Essentially, we distinguish between angled hatching, cross-hatching and dotted hatching.

Diagonal hatching, whether simple or crosshatched, is intended to emphasise the <u>flatness</u> of a building part or to indicate that part of a building lies in shadow. Then the lines of the hatching run in the direction of the light source. If simple hatching is made vertically or horizontally this can also indicate the material to be used. > Fig. 21, page 28 It is also possible to make hatching denser at an edge or corner as a way of depicting curvature. ∎

∎ **Tip:** Hatching ought not to be drawn too rapidly. Snaking thin lines, irregular distances between the lines or changes in direction give an impression of carelessness. The individual lines of the hatching should be drawn right up to the borders of the area to which the hatching is applied. This calls for patience and precision but it is the only way to achieve the desired effect, the depiction of a flat area.

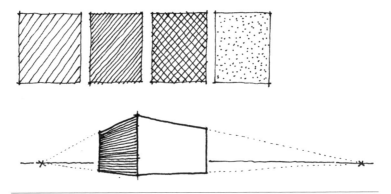

Fig. 18: Different kinds of hatching, in the perspective the hatching lines recede towards a vanishing point

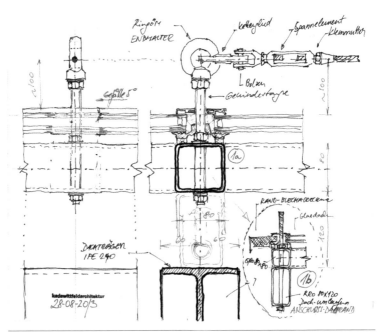

Fig. 19: Detail drawings (sections and isometric) of a facade construction with different line types and hatching

Fig. 20: Pencils, clutch pencils, graphite stick, eraser, sharpener and cutting knife

Pencils

The lead pencil, which is actually made of graphite with a clay binder that is encased in wood, is one of the most important sketching tools. It is undemanding, fast and flexible, economically priced and resistant to ageing. It is a sensitive drawing medium: you can draw both quick sketches and detailed studies with it. A low amount of <u>pressure</u> on the pencil creates a fine line that has a searching character. Once the perfect line has been found you can, using the same pencil, increase the pressure to produce a more definite line.

For sketching the most suitable pencils are grades B to 4B (soft to medium soft, B standing for black). The grading ranges from 8H (very hard) to H, HB (normal), B to 8B. If you use pencils of different hardness (or fineliners with different line thicknesses) in the same drawing, the difference in emphasis can produce a lively depiction. In general such drawings seem to have greater variety, but the beginner is advised to use just one pencil in a drawing. In this way you can begin to achieve full mastery of the pencil, whereas changing pencils during drawing reduces spontaneity and interrupts the important continuity of the drawing process.

As well as the classic wood pencil there are also propelling pencils. <u>Clutch pencils</u> have the same leads as pencils and are therefore also suitable for drawing. They are also available with very strong leads (approx. 6 mm thick) and these resemble graphite sticks, whose thick lead is covered only by a plastic coat. <u>Graphite sticks</u> can be used to draw flat areas. Fine propelling pencils should not be used, as their extremely thin leads do not allow different line thicknesses or heavy finger pressure. They are

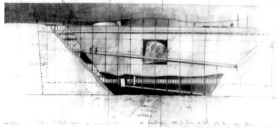

Fig. 21: Tchoban Foundation, Museum for Architectural Drawing, Berlin

Fig. 22: Design for a weather station

more suitable for technical drawing. As, after a time, using a drawing instrument that is too short causes cramps in the hand, an extender should
■ be attached to a pencil when half of it has been used up.

The eraser should be as white and soft as possible but at the same time it should have distinct edges so that lines can be properly removed. Blurring, that is rubbing lines and hatching with the finger, sheet or handkerchief should be avoided. Every individual line, even in close hatching,
■ should remain visible.

■ **Tip:** If the complete drawing can be approximately imagined before the first line is drawn it is worthwhile, if you are right handed, to begin the drawing at the top left and to end in the direction of bottom right (for a left-hander from top right to bottom left). This prevents smudging the drawing surface with your hand. This applies to pencils, charcoal sticks and pastels.

■ **Tip:** A (cutter) knife should be used to sharpen pencils or coloured pencils, as it can produce a very long exposed lead. This lasts for a long time and does not have to be re-sharpened during the drawing. If you regard it as important to have a lead point that remains the same, then a standard pencil sharpener will also do.

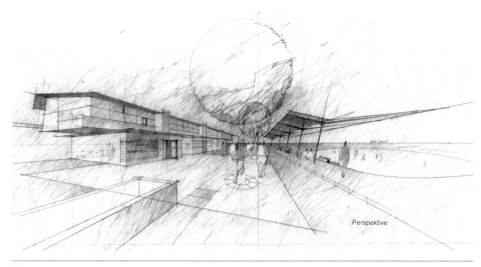

Fig. 23: Design perspective: a world of colour produced by combining different coloured pencils

Coloured pencils

Coloured pencils are made in the same way as normal pencils. A pressed lead made of colour pigment is encased in wood. They are also sensitive to pressure, allowing deep and light shades of a hue to be produced with the one pencil.

For sketching, 15–20 different colours are generally sufficient, as coloured pencils can also be combined with each other. In sketching they are particularly suitable for making the first colour concepts or for indications and information; in the later design process the use of coloured ■ pencils creates atmosphere and liveliness.

Felt pens

There is an extremely large range of different felt pens (also fibre pens, fineliners etc.). Essentially, all kinds of felt pens can be used for sketching and drawing; the fine differences are only revealed in the detail. Thicker felt pens are more suitable for freehand sketching; thin pens (up to 1 mm point thickness) are also suitable for drawings made with the use of a ruler and stencils.

> ■ **Tip:** Wooden planking can be depicted by parallel lines of red, brown, blue and green made with coloured pencils. A metallic surface is produced by combining lines of blue, green and grey.

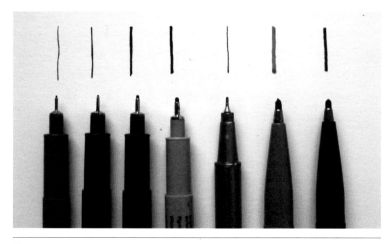

Fig. 24: Ink pens with different line widths and felt-tip pens

In choosing felt pens, solubility in water is an important criterion (e.g. on contact with watercolours). Water-resistant felt tip pens such as pigment ink pens are also fade-resistant. They can be obtained in different thicknesses and therefore resemble ink drawing instruments from the technical drawing field (DIN 15). Water-soluble felt pens are available in many different colours and can be used to show design changes or re-workings, or for general notes.

Ballpoint pens

Ballpoint pens produce lines by means of a small ball that transfers the viscous ink in the pen to the paper. The ballpoint is a pressure-sensitive drawing tool: if the pressure is increased a thicker line is produced, and if less pressure is used the line is thinner. This variety of line thicknesses makes the ballpoint suitable for depicting spatial volumes.

The ballpoint pen is an undemanding and speedy drawing tool. It can be used on all sorts of paper, but the hard ceramic surface of the ball makes it difficult to use on thin sketching paper. Only lines produced with document-quality ballpoint pens are resistant to ageing and do not change their appearance.

HAUS RODENBERG 17/06

Fig. 25: Ink pigment drawing using different line thicknesses to emphasise the volumes of the building, felt pens used to indicate shadow

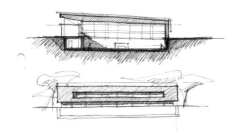

Fig. 26: Design drawing (section and elevation) made with a ballpoint pen

STAATSTHEATER 20/08

Fig. 27: On-site drawing made with a ballpoint pen

Fig. 28: Solid tone (opaque), halftone (transparent) and structured surface

SURFACES AND THE INSTRUMENTS FOR DRAWING THEM
Areas

A great deal can be achieved with pure line drawings, but some situations require instruments that can create flat areas or surfaces. If surfaces are used in part of a sketch it stands out very clearly from the rest of the drawing.

Hatching, which consists of individual lines, comes very close to a drawing made with surfaces. But making hatching can be extremely tedious and time-consuming. In addition, hatching only achieves monochrome suggestions of space or the nature of a material. In contrast, the implements for creating surface areas can be used rapidly, and using multiple tone values can heighten the depiction of space. Materials and surfaces can be drawn in a way that is much closer to nature, while a number of the instruments used to create surface areas can produce more authentic shadows.

Types of surfaces

It is far easier to distinguish between different types of lines than types of surfaces, as the latter are almost always tied to the kind of instrument used. However, the difference between solid tones, halftones and structured surfaces is important. > Fig. 28

Solid tone surfaces are surfaces that are drawn with full tonal value and are therefore opaque. Halftone surfaces do not have a full tonal value, are not opaque and therefore have a transparent quality. They seem predestined for use in depicting shadows. With structured surfaces the white of the paper may appear through at certain places. This has to do directly with the instrument being used. Common to all instruments used to create surfaces or areas is that they do not produce any visible lines.

Fig. 29: Form studies (pastels)

Pastels and charcoal sticks

Structured surfaces can be drawn with pastel chalks and charcoal sticks. The uneven abrasion on the paper creates interesting structures, which frequently have the appearance of stone surfaces. Due to their porosity, drawings made with pastels or charcoal must be given a coat of fixative.

Grey and brown pastels are generally sold in boxes. They are available in black, white, ochre, sepia, red chalk, and various shades of grey. A special effect can be achieved when thcy arc used on paper other than white. > Chapter Tools and techniques, Drawing substrates The rough quality of pastel drawings makes it necessary to use large sheets of paper. They are particularly useful during the early design stages for making studies of form, light and shadow. The hard contrasts produced by the full tone colours give the drawings a particularly dramatic quality. > Fig. 1 below left, page 8 ■

■ **Tip:** Brown and grey pastels are often only 7 mm thick, with a length of approx. 8 cm. Therefore it is a good idea to break them into pieces 2–3 cm long before using them. This makes them easier to handle and also means that, in addition to the short end, the other side, which is then not so long, can also be used to create flat areas of colour.

Fig. 30: Neue Pinakothek Munich sequences (charcoal pencil)

Fat-free <u>charcoal pencils</u> are available in different degrees of hardness. Their great advantage is that they can be easily used when one is on the move as they have the same form as the standard pencil and therefore are not so easily broken. They produce a very dense black that allows strong contrasts to be made. Charcoal drawings are generally highly expressive and particularly effective for depicting cubic, voluminous buildings. Charcoal pencils are somewhere between line and surface drawing instruments. They produce lines that are very thick and clear, but it is also very easy to create surfaces and structures, for example of masonry, with them.

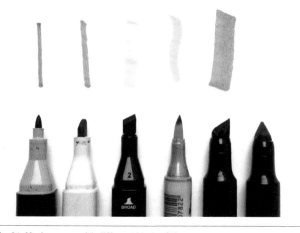

Fig. 31: Marker pens with different kinds of tips

Marker pens

Alcohol-based marker pens are excellent for indicating colour, materials and shadows when drawing and sketching architecture. Sketches coloured with marker pens have a vivid spatial quality. You have to work very fast with markers as the sketch dries almost immediately.

Most alcohol-based marker pens have drawing tips at either end of the pen, which have a different shape and degree of hardness. There are softer brush tips, with which one can work in a painterly way, and harder wedge or trapezoid-shaped tips that can be used to create areas of colour or lines of different thicknesses.

They are available in several hundred colours; however you really only need various warm and cold shades of grey, a lighter and a darker red, green, blue and yellow, as well as a few brown and beige shades, and of course black. Marker colours are often stronger than you might think. Before sketching, the shade of colour should be tested. To create different shades of a colour, a <u>blender pen</u> is needed that dissolves the colour of the marker by means of a solvent.

○

○ **Note:** The blender pen (frequently called: "0") can lighten an area of colour at any required place or at the edges. A colour gradient is obtained by first applying the required colour with a marker pen to a smooth surface (e.g. a sheet of glass). The colour is then taken up by the blender. The colour gradient is now drawn, the colour initially appearing in full tone and then gradually thinning out to transparent white.

Fig. 32: Design sketch with markers, using different colour gradients

Fig. 33: Design fantasy, pencil coloured with marker pens, drawn on special paper with shadows depicted transparently

Alcohol-based marker pens can be used on many different kinds of paper. However, standard, open-pored paper absorbs a lot of the marker colour, giving the drawing a more powerful quality. In sketchbooks a rough sheet of paper must be inserted between the page being used and the next one to prevent the colour soaking through. For drawing areas of colour smooth papers are most suitable, for instance the roll of sketching paper.

Fig. 34: Kolumba Cologne, purely marker pen drawing, made on site

Drawings made exclusively with marker pens have a particularly three-dimensional and atmospheric effect. Here one works from the lightest to the darkest layer of a "family" of markers (e.g. warm shades of grey). At those parts of the building that face towards the light the white of the paper should be allowed to shine through, without a layer of marker ink. ■

■ **Tip:** Materiality can also be excellently depicted with marker pens. Horizontal or vertical clapboard cladding can be shown by minimal overlapping of the individual lines drawn with the broad, trapezoid-shaped tip of the pen. The overlapping creates darker areas of the colour used, which suggests the shadow joints between the wooden boards. Concrete surfaces are often vertically structured at their upper and lower ends due to weathering. This impression can be created with the tip of the light grey marker. The outlines of the individual formwork panels and the turnbuckles are drawn with darker grey.

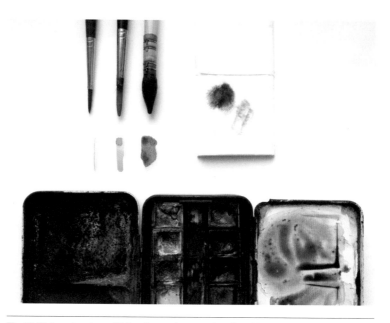

Fig. 35: Watercolour box with brushes and a paper handkerchief as absorbent surface

Watercolours

In some cases it is essential to show the colour of the parts of a building, the vegetation or the sky. This can be in an architectural design or while making drawings of existing architecture on the move. Watercolours enable you to depict the colouring of materials, atmosphere and nature in a realistic way.

A (metal) watercolour box is the most suitable; the standard kinds available generally have between 12 and 24 colour pans. However, all you really need are the primary colours yellow, red and blue (not necessarily the richest shades) and 1–2 natural shades of green, a brown and an ochre shade, and black. Brushes should be the series 4, 12 and 24. A larger watercolour box may also have a surface on which to mix colours and a compartment to store the brushes so that they are protected against fraying.

Watercolours generally take the form of pressed, dried colour pigments with which different shades or intensities of a basic colour can be obtained by mixing them with water. This mixing also gives the watercolour a glazing, i.e. translucent, quality. Layers of watercolour can be placed one on top of the other, provided you have the necessary patience, as you must wait until one layer has dried before applying the next one, if you wish to avoid the new colour blending with the earlier one. In using watercolours you generally work from light to dark areas on the sheet. At the brightest part of the drawing there should be no layer of watercolour, just the white of the paper. > Fig. 38 Monochrome watercolours are also fascinating.

The translucent quality of watercolour paints makes them suitable for depicting shadows. You do not always have to use a watercolour based on black that depicts shadows as a grey film and darkens the area of colour beneath it. Depending on the particular mood of the drawing, shadows can also be made using dark violet, dark blue or dark green hues.

A colour gradient to depict vaulted areas or the sky can be easily produced using watercolours. First the basic colour required is mixed. The area that will finally have the deepest colour is painted first; this is generally done with a size 12 brush. Then the brush is very gently washed in a glass of water and excess water equally gently removed by using a paper handkerchief. The brush still holds the same colour, but the intensity is slightly reduced. Now painting is continued on the still wet paper, again covering only a small area at a time. This procedure is repeated until the entire area required is painted or until the brush holds water only, without any trace of colour. ■

■ **Tip:** If you are painting larger areas with watercolours it is helpful to raise the sheet on the side further away from you. The colour mix should be applied downwards, causing it to flow towards you. Watercolour is applied until the lower edge of the painted area is formed in the shape of a long drop. Then brush can be filled again with colour and continued at the area already painted without creating any visible edges or lines.

Fig. 36: Monochrome design watercolour

Fig. 37: Depicting curved or vaulted surfaces with watercolours
requires the use of colour gradients.

A pencil drawing coloured with watercolours is a delightful mix. Generally, it is difficult to draw in pencil on coarse, thick, <u>watercolour paper</u> and therefore a smoother paper must be used, but this does not easily allow several layers of watercolour to be applied. A compromise is necessary. As few as possible layers of colour should be applied in order to avoid damaging the paper. On this account this technique is not a pure

Fig. 38: Sketched, naturalistic colours of a building and its surroundings

watercolour but a colouring. The use of watercolours allows the important things to be easily separated from the unimportant, and the composition is simplified. When not all of the drawing is coloured and it thus becomes clear where the focus lies, the concentration makes the depiction more interesting. ■ ○

■ **Tip:** If using watercolours while on the move it is useful to carry with you a small screw-top jar filled with water. Paper handkerchiefs can be used to dry the brush and to clean the box after drawing.

○ **Note:** Watercolours are not only available in the form of compressed colour blocks. Watercolour pencils look much the same as normal coloured pencils but are water-soluble and can be painted over with water later. Liquid artists watercolours in tubes offer more intense colours than the blocks, but they are complicated to mix on palettes and therefore not so suitable for rapid freehand drawing.

Fig. 39: On-site drawing made with ink pen and watercolour pencils, later given a water wash

Fig. 40: Pencil drawing with watercolours: a classic in the illustration of architecture (building site Grossmarkthalle Frankfurt am Main)

SPECIAL INSTRUMENTS USED IN ARCHITECTURAL DESIGN
Triangular scales

The triangular (architect's) scale is a drawing and measuring tool, about 30 cm long, with which one can draw and measure lines at different scales. It is an indispensable tool in architectural design. On each of the three faces there are two different scales, giving a total of six usable scales. Each edge is allocated to a particular scale or pair of scales (e.g. 1:2, 1:5, 1:10, 1:20, 1:25, 1:33, 1:50, 1:75, 1:100, 1:125, 1:150, 1:200, 1:250, 1:500 or 1:1000).

Triangular scales can be made of plastic or aluminium. If buying one you should ensure that it has as many possible different scales as possible. Of course, the scale 1:2 can be easily converted to use for drawings at a scale of 1:20 and 1:200 and so forth.

A triangular scale is placed on a scale design sketch in order to determine the scale, to check a particular dimension in the sketch, or to change a dimension. The triangular scale is also suitable for measuring existing plans or drawings that have no dimensions, but whose scale is known. If you draw freely without any existing basis you can draw the desired length in metres directly to the desired scale.

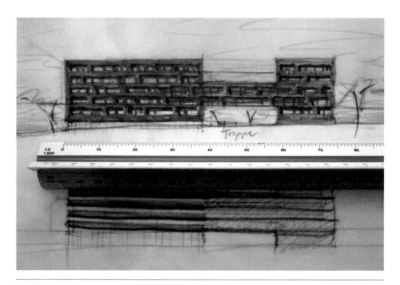

Fig. 41: Measuring a sketched elevation (scale 1:500) with the triangular scale

Fig. 42: Ruler, set square, triangular scale, French curve, circle template

Rulers, set squares and templates

Rulers and set squares can be used to check rapidly made sketches to see whether their dimensions and proportions need to be developed further. Straight-edge rulers produce mono-dimensional drawings. Their disadvantage is that they are suitable only for drawing straight lines. They are, however, ideal for constructing perspectives with one or more vanishing points. > Fig. 23, page 29 The transparent <u>set square</u>, which is also used for technical drawing, is very useful for drawing parallels and lines at right angles, or any other angle required, to a given line. The length of the hypotenuse (the long side of the triangle) should be 32 cm. A grip makes this implement easier to use.

<u>French curves</u> are available as prefabricated stencils. They come from the field of mathematics, where they are used to draw parabolas and functions. In architecture they are particularly useful for drawing round design elements, especially in perspective. If a particular curve is not available a flexible curve can be used. A <u>circle template</u> with circles of different diameters is always useful.

Freehand drawing in architectural design

DRAWING TYPES

Generations of architects have debated and examined which form of illustration is most suitable for conveying an impression of their building to themselves and to different groups of people. Looking at the depictions of architecture as described in contracts and the basic forms of depiction used by architects work we find the following range of drawings: site plan, floor plan, elevation, section, detail, perspective and then, less commonly, axonometric. Architects use these drawings to express different aspects of their designs. These aspects can be roughly broken down into the following architectural categories: the urban situation, the function, the construction, the proportions, the configuration of building volumes, the way the building parts fit together, and the materials used in the building. This applies to technical drawings made to a particular scale as well as to freehand sketches, which at the start of a design are generally made without any scale. When the design becomes more concrete or when the planning commission is based on an existing building, the freehand sketches also employ a scale. You discover which drawing at which scale is ideal for conveying the intended content through individual experience and by drawing regularly. Designs should be continually developed and examined in several types of drawings.

Site plan, floor plan, section and elevation are planar depictions, i.e. simple projections. They are not experienced in reality, as the elevation, for instance, is an "unrealistic" drawing, made at right angles to the building from an infinite distance. We experience a real building very differently. The site plan and elevation describe the exterior of a building, while the floor plan and section provide mostly information about the internal configuration of the building. Axonometric projections are based on planar depictions but also show the third dimension, height. Perspectives are central projections and are based on one or more vanishing points.

Pictogram

Pictograms are a special case. These are symbolic graphics that attempt only to convey the design idea or design variations. They must not be based on any of the drawing types referred to above and must not provide any concrete information or data about the design. The drawn form of the pictogram is very free, but generally extremely clear in graphical terms. They do not use any scale. > Fig. 44

Fig. 43: Sketches of different projections: floor plan, section, elevations (developed design)

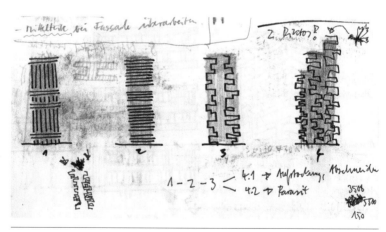

Fig. 44: Pictograms of different facade versions (conversion of an existing high-rise)

Fig. 45: Site plan with neighbouring buildings and a perspective
with the first impression of the exterior

Site plan

The largest scale drawing of an individual building or complex of buildings is the site plan. The site plan shows the location of all building parts
on the site and its immediate surroundings, whose surface areas are also
shown. The building that is the subject of the design is shown as a <u>top
view</u>. Site plans are generally drawn at a scale of 1:500, at earlier design
stages and in larger building projects also at 1:1000.

It makes sense also to show the immediate surroundings of the
planned building. These can include neighbouring buildings, vegetation
or infrastructure elements. Site plans often contain legends, levels (height
above sea level) and arrows that indicate entrances or circulation. North
is generally to the top of the sheet, a <u>north arrow</u> (or pointer) should
always be used. The building should be drawn in such a way that it stands
out clearly from the surrounding developments. This can be achieved by
heightening the contrast, by using thicker lines, or by the use of colour
or surface textures. > Figs. 36, page 40, and 45 The site boundaries are indicated with a dashed line. > Figs. 46 and 47

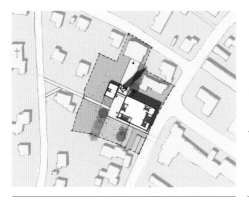

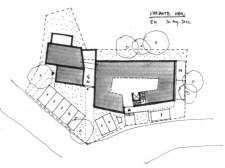

Fig. 46: Immediate surroundings highlighted by use of coloured areas on the computer

Fig. 47: Schematic ground floor plan with depiction of the site

Floor plan

A floor plan is a horizontal cut through a building. Architects always look down from above, that is to say, a cut is made through the building and everything that can be seen below the line of the cut is shown. This line is chosen so that all the openings and the circulation systems can be seen. The floor plan shows the <u>arrangement of rooms</u> on the different floors, each floor being drawn separately. Floor plans reveal spatial sequences and functions. Sketches of ground floor plans should show the nature of the surrounding area of the site.

Dark or black-coloured walls outlining white rooms are one of the principal characteristics of a floor plan sketch. They reveal the <u>building typology</u>, separate rooms from each other, or indicate the structural system. In the early stages of the design the floor plan sketches do not yet have these typical characteristics. In such cases, simple coloured areas may be used to indicate sequences of spaces that will eventually provide the configuration of the building. > Fig. 48 Floor plans of this type are generally at a scale of 1:200. In the later planning stages floor plans must ■ be drawn at scales of up to 1:50.

■ **Tip:** If the shape or position of the further floors of the building differs from the floor plan shown it makes sense to indicate them using full, dashed or dotted lines (see Chapter Tools and techniques, Lines and the instruments for drawing them).

Fig. 48: A floor plan takes shape through the arrangement of rooms, sorted by colour according to their function.

Fig. 49: Sketch section at the design stage with depiction of the surroundings

Section

The section is made by placing a vertical section plane in the design on which everything that you see when looking in a specific horizontal direction is then depicted. The section plane should be chosen in such a way that all the important room heights, the way the structure works and the circulation of the building can be read. What lies close to the section plane is drawn clearly; building parts that are further away can be drawn more lightly in elevation. > Fig. 50

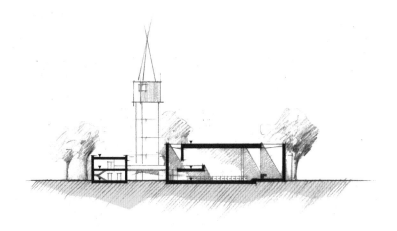

Fig. 50: Sectional drawing made at the design stage showing surrounding buildings and trees

During the early design phases the sketched section is a most important means of illustration. Often it is needed in order to clarify decisive spatial situations. The scale of building sections and elevations depends on how far the design of the floor plans has advanced. If the floor plans are drawn at a scale of 1:100 it makes sense to draw the sections and elevations at this scale too. Urban planning sections through terrain are generally drawn at a scale of 1:500.

To grasp the complexity of a building a number of sections are generally needed (at least one cross section and one longitudinal section). As with the floor plan the walls and ceiling slabs cut through are coloured dark or crosshatched, and important edges that are not directly visible are indicated by dashed or dotted lines. The position of the top of the surrounding terrain should be shown in every section and is depicted by a strong line. If the design involves changing this level the original edge of the terrain can be shown as a dashed line. Elements that provide a sense of scale, such as people, vehicles and vegetation, give section and elevation drawings a certain lively quality and make them easier to read.

> Chapter Freehand drawing in architectural design, Indicators of scale

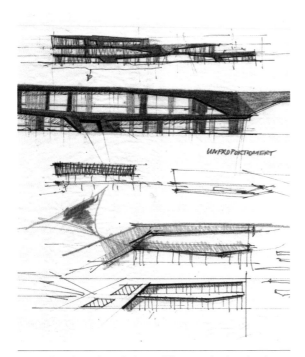

Fig. 51: Elevations of one design at different scales in a sketch

Elevation

The elevation (or view) is a planar drawing that shows one external face of a building. It could be regarded as a sectional drawing in which, however, the section plane is not inside the building but outside and directly in front of it. The elevation depicts the proportions of a design or reveals the relationship of the planned building to its surroundings (neighbouring buildings, nature etc.). The relief of a building (facade, windows, projections) should also be visible and can be shown by means of shadows. This gives an essentially planar drawing such an elevation a certain depth. Building parts in the background are, as in the section, drawn more faintly and with separated lines.

During architectural design the elevation can be sketched directly beside, above, or below a plan drawing, as the lengths required are already given. It is important that the ground line on which the building stands be emphasised, and that the planned building be clearly distinguished in the drawing from the neighbouring buildings.

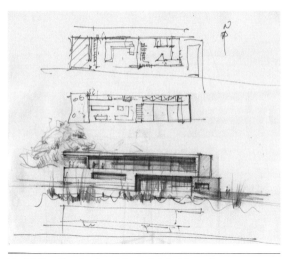

Fig. 52: Elevation developed from sketched floor plans

Detail

If you wish to define the construction or materials of a building precisely, you must proceed to drawing at a smaller scale. What are called the details of the building are shown in section, elevation or perspective drawings. Particularly important are detail sketches of those places where the different parts of the building are pieced together, where materials meet, where construction meets design. The term "detail drawing" can cover drawings made at very different scales. A very detailed depiction at the scale of 1:1 to 1:5 is clearly a detail, but so is the depiction of a facade at the scale of 1:50, as this offers far more detailed information than the scale normally used for an elevation drawing.

In detail sketches it may be necessary to define certain materials precisely. There are standards that lay down the kind of hatching or lines used to depict materials. In a large-scale section the cut building parts are indicated by thicker lines. To allow visual checks to be made frequently, a part of the relevant internal and external elevation and a floor plan are drawn alongside the detail section drawing (vertical or horizontal section).

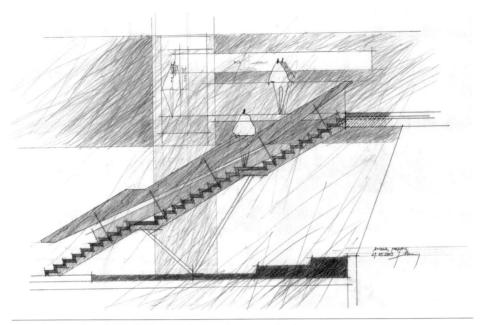

Fig. 53: Large-scale staircase detail with indication of colours and materials

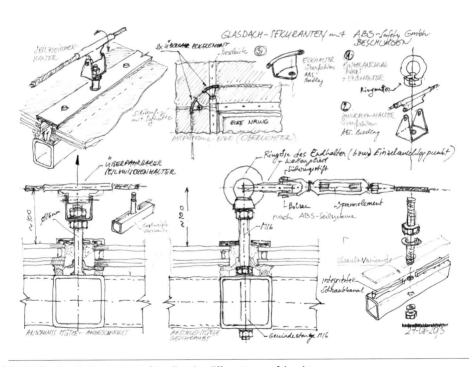

Fig. 54: Small-scale development of details using different types of drawing

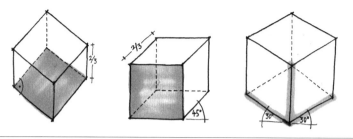

Fig. 55: Floor plan axonometric, elevation axonometric and isometric projection.

Axonometric projections

Axonometric projections combine the advantages of planar and three-dimensional drawings as they combine both kinds of depictions: in some kinds of axonometric projections, the depths and heights of rooms can be measured from the drawing. These drawings are frequently used in the architect's daily life to depict simple spatial relationships. They are often based on existing drawings and in such cases adopt the scales of these drawings. The three simplest and most common axonometric projections used in architectural design are the floor plan axonometric, the elevation axonometric, and the isometric projection. > Fig. 55

The floor plan axonometric projection (or military projection) is based on the floor plan, i.e. the dimensions of the floor plan are retained and can read off the constructed axonometric projection. The heights are generally reduced by one third. If a floor plan drawing of a current design already exists, then a spatial depiction can be very quickly drawn using a roll of sketching paper. The disadvantage of the floor plan axonometric is the large visible surface of the top view.

The floor plan axonometric as an exploded drawing (which can also be made on the basis of an isometric) is very informative but relatively time-consuming. Here, the different floors, building parts or planes of the construction are shown separated from each other but linked by connecting lines and by the geometric severity of the axonometric projection.

The elevation axonometric projection (also sometimes called cavalier projection) is based on the elevation. The elevation of the building is viewed frontally; the volume develops behind it at an angle. The depth of the building volume is shortened, generally by a third or a half. This form of axonometric projection is easy to produce if an elevation of the design is already available.

54

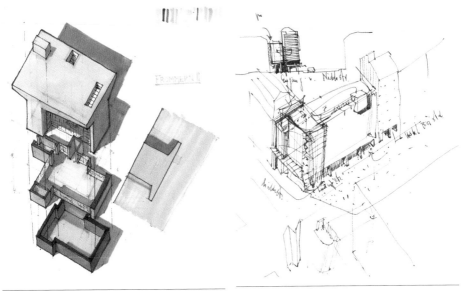

Fig. 56: Floor plan axonometric projection as an exploded drawing

Fig. 57: Rapidly sketched isometric to explain a spatial situation, with elevation

The isometric ("iso" comes from the ancient Greek and means equal) offer true lengths in all directions, however the floor plan is distorted and shown without a right angle. Therefore the isometric cannot be made on the basis of an existing drawing. > Chapter Freehand drawing in architectural design, Continuing the design But the additional effort involved in making this kind of drawing is worthwhile, as the isometric has the illustrative character of a bird's eye view. The isometric is often used in drawing overview plans.

Free perspectives

A perspective drawing differs in one important point from the floor plan, elevation, section and axonometric: it has one or more vanishing points. That is to say parallel edges, building parts or buildings are not drawn parallel to each other but meet at a vanishing point. Perspectives are particularly suitable for making a building understandable in a clear, communicative way that lay people can grasp. Such perspectives are often drawn from the eye level of someone passing by a building, as the aim is to depict spatial impressions realistically. In addition to the outer spatial configuration, the perspective also shows particularly clearly the form and proportions of a building and how it is integrated in urban design.
> Fig. 39, page 42

In situations in which designs based on planar drawings such as floor plan, section and elevation must be quickly examined in spatial terms,

Fig. 58: Rapidly drawn perspective (not constructed) at the height of a passer-by for an urban design ideas competition

Fig. 59: Sectional perspectives of sports halls

bird's eye perspectives, sectional perspectives and perspectivised elevations are used. These are rarely based on the laws that govern the construction of perspectives but nevertheless communicate the design idea.

In the <u>perspective that a lay person can easily read</u>, the horizon, which in such rapidly made perspectives is generally not drawn, usually lies in the area of the ground floor of the building. This creates the illusion of a realistic passer-by's view of a building in its spatial setting, whether this is the city or the country.

<u>Bird's eye perspectives</u> are three-dimensional drawings looking down from the sky, i.e. the station point of the perspective is above the

building. Like the site plan they show both the building and its surroundings. You see a distorted top view of the building itself and at least one elevation. > Fig. 37, page 40

The combination of section and perspective known as the <u>sectional perspective</u> is a most communicative form of depiction. It can show the architectural characteristics known from the section, while giving the drawing a spatial dimension.

The <u>perspectivised elevation</u> suggests, in perspective, an area in front of a building, and in this way counteracts the absence of perspective in a classic elevation. > Fig. 43 below, page 46, and Fig. 45, page 47 As long as the elevation does not suffer in graphical terms, it can improve the otherwise rather abstract elevation of a building.

Constructed perspective

Freely drawn perspectives cannot always completely satisfy or convince the designer and the viewer, as they are not geometrically constructed and are consequently imprecise. To produce a correct perspective, even in freehand drawing, a construction method that comes from descriptive geometry can be used. The basis of this method is shown below for an orthogonal building, using two vanishing points.

To construct a perspective in this way you require a floor plan and at least one elevation of the design. These drawings must be put on the paper, at the same scale, before the perspective is constructed – in the form of a sketch, copy or print. Ideally, however, the perspective should be drawn on transparent paper; the drawings referred to above can be placed beneath the transparent sheet. > Fig. 64, page 60

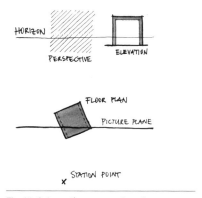

Fig. 60: Schematic construction of a
perspective (the perspective will be drawn
in the crosshatched area)

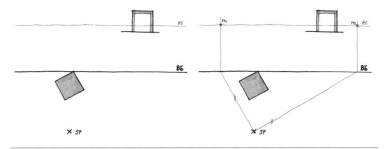

Fig. 61: Preparation and construction of the vanishing points

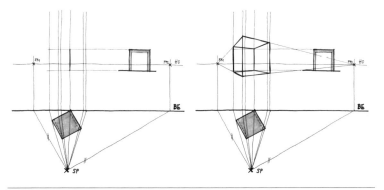

Fig. 62: Transfer of the true height and construction of the perspective

On the sheet the perspective is constructed from bottom to top. Near the bottom edge of the sheet is the station point (SP). Now the floor plan must be positioned in such a way that the desired perspective can be drawn. The distance to the station point must be determined, and the floor plan must be swivelled until an interesting view is found. The elevation is placed above the floor plan, not centrally but to the left or right of the floor plan. The perspective is created alongside the elevation and above the floor plan. The picture plane (PP) is drawn through the floor plan as a horizontal line, parallel to the ground line of the elevation. Its position determines the size of the final perspective. Ideally it should be positioned so that it cuts at least one important corner or edge of the building. In the elevation drawing the vertical position of the horizon (HO) is chosen. It is drawn parallel to the ground line of the elevation and to the picture plane in the upper part of the sheet. > Fig. 60

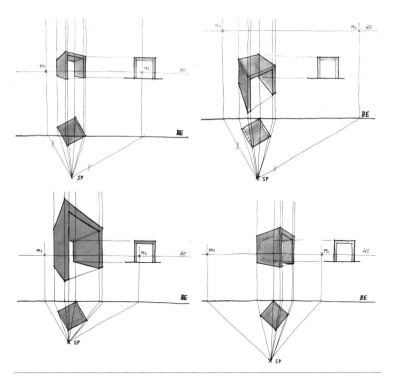

Fig. 63: Changing the position of the picture plane, the horizon and the station point and swivelling the building

This preparatory work should be carried out before constructing the perspective. Now the vanishing points needed are constructed. To do this lines are drawn parallel to the orthogonal outside edges of the floor plan and are extended to meet the picture plane. At each of the points where they meet this plane a vertical line is drawn up to the horizon. These two new points are the two vanishing points. > Fig. 61

○

○ **Note:** Although this construction method is relatively time consuming it produces only a small perspective. It also requires a good understanding of the procedure and the variables. Only the main principles are presented in this book. Construction methods employing one or three vanishing points are not dealt with, nor are the construction of shadows or perspectives of non-orthogonal floor plans.

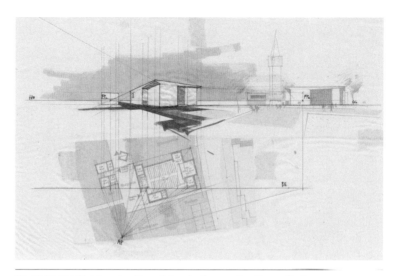

Fig. 64: Perspective based on the point projection construction method

In the next step the building volume is transferred from the plan to the perspective to be drawn. To do this lines are drawn from the station point to the important corner points of the building in plan and continued to the picture plane. From these points on the picture verticals are drawn. Here the corner point of the floor plan that cuts the picture plane should also be included. Only at those points where the plan drawing cuts the picture plane can <u>real heights</u> be transferred from the elevation to the perspective.

Now the perspective can be created step by step. From the first edge of the building vanishing lines are drawn to the next building edge, the position of which has been defined by the verticals already drawn. Seen from the eye-point the right-hand sides of the building sides always vanish to the right vanishing point and left-hand sides to the left vanishing point. > Fig. 62

In this method, four <u>variables</u> determine the appearance of the constructed perspective. > Fig. 63 If you change the position of the picture plane in relation to the floor plan this changes the size of the drawing. Only those building parts on the picture plane retain their size. The horizon determines the vertical height of the station point. If the elevation drawing cuts the horizon you obtain a view of the building from above or below. Shifting the station point immediately changes the perspective. If it is close to (far from) the floor plan the perspective can seem very dramatic (flat). If the floor plan is turned until it reaches the desired position in relation to the station point, this changes the position of the vanishing points. > Fig. 63

INDICATORS OF SCALE

In the technical architectural drawing – such as the floor plan – familiar forms for <u>fittings</u> or <u>furnishings</u> such as toilets, staircases or doors serve as a scale that gives the viewer a grasp of the proportions. These indicators of scale are enormously important for the outside viewer, whether clients, colleagues or lay people. They should be included in all architectural drawings –both the architectural design and the drawing made on site. They also include drawings of <u>trees</u> and <u>plants</u>, <u>people</u>, <u>street furniture</u>, <u>vehicles</u>, and in some cases also the <u>sky</u>.

People

Showing people in architectural drawings is of great importance. They give the virtual building a vertical <u>dimension</u> that everyone can immediately understand. They are indispensable above all in elevations and sections; > Fig. 49, page 49 and in perspectives passers-by or users of the building dimension the space that the design intends to convey. > Fig. 23, page 29 They are more rarely found in floor plans where they are not obligatory. The manner in which people are depicted depends on whether they accompany the design in an additive manner or are intended to indicate how the space is dimensioned. Like everything else people can be depicted in a variety of ways. > Figs. 15, 53, 58, 74 and 90

Views of architecture drawn on site can also be given a scale by adding people. If these drawings are perspectives then, before starting to draw, you should consider your position relative to other people. If you stand when drawing then (assuming a straight plane) the heads of all standing adults should be shown on the horizon line, no matter how near or far away they are. > Fig. 74, page 72 Here, too, you are confronted with the basic decision about what level of importance should be given to the people depicted. The main focus should always be on the architecture.

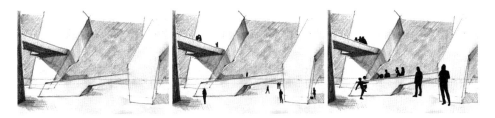

Fig. 65: A sketch of a space initially without dimensions. Attempts to dimension it with different depictions of people give the space very different sizes.

Fig. 66: Trees as positive and negative, the focus is on the composition as a whole

Vegetation

Where they seem relevant in a drawing, <u>trees</u> can be depicted in many different ways. There are innumerable kinds of trees and many of them change their appearance with the seasons. How one depicts trees is always a question of the composition or the focal point on the sheet. If the attention is to be directed to a building that is surrounded by trees, these should be drawn faintly and vaguely. > Fig. 50, page 50 If the drawing is intended more to convey an overall impression, the trees and the building can be given roughly equal emphasis. > Fig. 66 Whatever the case, the depiction of vegetation helps to integrate the architecture into its established setting. > Fig. 25, page 31 Trees should not be drawn too small, as this makes the building appear proportionally too large.

To make a (deciduous) tree appear more three-dimensional in summer the mass of leaves with the trunk should first of all be shown as an outline drawing. The trunk and the branches can be added, but it is more important to break the tree up into so-called "leaf-clouds" whose structure is more defined on their shadow side. It should be noted that "leaf-clouds" that have one side in shadow and one in the light appear more three-dimensional. > Fig. 10, page 18, and Fig. 27, page 31 Conversely, in winter trees consist only of the structure of the trunk and the branches, which grow thinner towards the top of the tree. In depicting trees a combination of line drawing (pencil or fineliner) with a number of surface areas (marker pen or watercolours) is particularly charming. > Fig. 36, page 40

Fig. 67: Different kinds of trees

Bushes, grass and other kinds of incidental <u>vegetation</u> should be indicated only by a variety of lines or suggestions of irregular textures, and should never be too dominant.

Vehicles

Much like architecture and the human body, motorised vehicles are made up almost exclusively of basic geometric shapes added together. Most of the parts of a car can therefore be constructed relatively simply in a drawing. In elevation and sections they are generally needed only in the form of silhouettes, but in perspectives they are three-dimensional volumes. In designs that stand on busy streets in particular, cars must be drawn so that they fit properly into the given space in terms of perspective – i.e. they must be drawn correctly with regard to the vanishing point. > Fig. 68

Sky

If the horizon (the horizon that actually describes the top of the visible land or building mass) can be seen on the sheet, the depiction of the sky acquires particular importance. Like almost everything else the sky can be depicted in a number of different ways. Hatching can convey a certain dramatic quality if the lines become denser towards the horizon or point towards a vanishing point. This effect can also be achieved by a gradient using watercolours or marker pens. Whatever the case, care should be taken that the upper area of <u>clouds</u> is not given any colour but

Fig. 68: Like the buildings, the car on the road vanishes towards the vanishing point.

is left white. Only the underside of the clouds should be depicted. > Fig. 38, page 41 The same applies when you hatch clouds: in the lower part of the cloud close to the horizon the hatching lines are condensed, and the upper part of the cloud is left untouched. A sky can be edged with nearby trees, neighbouring buildings or electricity wires, no matter whether it is just hatched or depicted with watercolours. Whether and in what way the sky is present in an elevation or a perspective can also supply information about the topographical surroundings of the site of the planned building.

Degree of abstraction

A floor plan at a scale of 1:100 is intended for a certain stage of the planning process (design planning). This scale also suggests that, in comparison to earlier planning stages, the drawing is larger in terms of the area of paper needed, and that more must be depicted. This could take the form of the way rooms are furnished, details of the construction or of the building services. In contrast in such plans the urban context will hardly be visible.

It is not only in the field of technical drawing that particular scales are allocated to the different planning stages. Freehand drawing should also obey certain rules in order to ensure that legibility is preserved, for lay people as well. This is a difficult topic to deal with as sketching is always dependent on the individual style and expression of the draughtsperson. Essentially, however, the size of the drawing should always match the content shown.

A design is often made on the basis of an existing drawing with a known scale. Where this is not the case, a triangular scale can help. Freehand sketches without a basis should not be too large, as they are generally used in the early planning stages where details have yet to be clarified.

In architectural drawing on site, the size of a perspective can greatly influence its expressive strength. People, vegetation, vehicles and urban furniture enrich every drawing through atmosphere and by suggesting dimensions. They function extremely well in terms of indicating scale, whereas other things tend to hinder the understanding of space. The depiction of individual stones in a wall or roof tiles from a great distance can strongly influence the apparent size. In addition, repetition of the same structures can often seem childish; it is far preferable merely to suggest such structures. As in the early planning stage of a design, a greater distance from the object being drawn demands a higher degree of abstraction.

CONTINUING THE DESIGN

Only the very first sketch of a design consists of pure thoughts, and every sketch that follows reacts to what has been drawn before by rejecting it, accepting it or developing it further. But sometime or other the point comes where the information in the sketches must be carried a step further. The sketch consolidates at a certain scale and finds the way from abstraction to concretisation.

The steps that a design has to undergo before it is realised are in principle comparable to the architect's services, as described in the professional scale of fees. During the basic evaluation, the design and approval plans and the later technical and economic design phases, the design constantly changes in the way it is depicted and, as a result, also changes the scale. The types of drawing that emerge show the design from all side and at different levels of depth, support it or reveal its flaws.

The freehand sketch reveals its advantages as a mediator between the different scales and planning stages. A drawing that previously only existed at a larger scale can be transferred to a different scale through the draughtsperson's experience. The visual language changes. At this stage, leave may be taken of the medium of freehand drawing in order to concretise and dimension the design by producing technical drawings. If what had been hoped for does not emerge as a result the sketch can be used again, which advances the design even though it involves going back a step in either scale or thought. This is how a design develops, through advances and setbacks, and the design method does not compete but switches between freehand and technical drawing, model and simulation, and engages with them in a meaningful symbiosis.

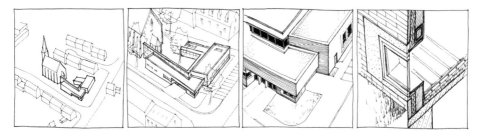

Fig. 69: Changing visual languages in consecutive design steps

Based on a printed-out photo of a model, the building volume can be examined using a roll of sketching paper. CAD applications often have axonometric view areas in which planar drawings such as floor plans or elevations can be shown in parallel perspective. If we print out this view area it can provide the basis for a useful and informative axonometric. > Fig. 56, page 55 Equally, a digitalised drawing can be imported into any CAD program. It is positioned so that it lies visibly on its own construction plane so that the lines conceived can be drawn over with vectors.

When the end of a design phase approaches and concrete results are required, the medium of freehand drawing need not be abandoned. For example, competition entries that use plans and perspectives drawn freehand stand out among many presentation plans made completely on the computer. Their authenticity gives the viewer the feel that the author has holistically engaged with his or her work. Hand-drawn details are just as suitable as CAD details to accompany the specifications for a particular trade. > Fig. 19, page 26 The points of contact between analogous and digital design media are numerous and varied.

Architectural drawing on site

The special thing about drawing on site – however banal it may sound – is <u>being present</u> in front of the architecture, its phenomenological appearance, observing the building directly and then transferring this to the drawing. Drawing on site means drawing an existing piece of architecture which our eyes see and which penetrates our brain and which, with our hand, we reproduce on a sheet of paper. This illustrates the difference both to design sketches, which are derived from the imagination, and to photography, which rarely works in a cognitive way.

Through the repeated act of looking closely, drawing on site encourages the development of a <u>building archive</u> in which patterns, geometries, structures, forms and typologies can be stored. The draughtsperson appropriates a building individually and produces a two-dimensional equivalent of the image that he or she has perceived, at an undefined scale. ■

DRAWING TYPES

When we look at a building on site, we find ourselves in a specific relationship to it in terms of perspective. This means that the <u>perspective</u> is the sole realistic type of drawing you can draw without a further examination of the building. This is the great difference from projection drawings. A site plan, an elevation, or an axonometric cannot be produced on site without walking around the building; you will not be able to draw an elevation correctly if you are not positioned at right angles to the building; you will not be able to draw a floor plan or a section if you have only looked at the building from outside.

■ **Tip:** A drawing that you have started on site should, wherever possible, also be finished on site. You should never draw from photographs as this prevents atmospheric and spatial impressions from appearing in the drawing, neglects some aspects and exaggerates others. Drawing on site offers an opportunity to refine your perception and therefore a chance to show by means of particular aspects what was important to you at the particular time. Nobody can assume another person's perception. Nevertheless the scene should also be photographed so that afterwards you can compare the reality with what you have perceived.

Fig. 70: Drawing excursion to Runkel: despite similar conditions and the same rules of drawing, individual drawing styles still emerge.

Fig. 71: Drawing excursion to Dietkirchen: the choice of drawing instruments influences the depiction.

However, since an architect uses a variety of methods of illustration in order to make certain ideas in the design understandable, you should attempt on site to make other drawings as well as perspectives. If, say, the focus of interest is on the construction of the building, you should try to make a section or draw a detail. However, this means you must first enter the building, walk around it and examine it closely. This inspection encourages the cognitive penetration of the building through understanding the logic of its structure.

PERSPECTIVE DRAWING

Someone who makes freehand drawings of real architecture cannot use the constructed perspective method as they do not have the floor plan and elevation needed. Nevertheless, by observing certain principles rules and laws it is still possible to draw a correct perspective. Perspective is particularly useful for the depiction of space. A measurable spatial depth, which is imitated in all perspectives, cannot be taken a freely drawn perspective, as perspectives do not have any scale.

The depiction of space is regulated by <u>five principles</u>:
1. The first principle of perspective illustration is that of the <u>spatial constant</u>. It describes the relationships between the sizes of objects in the depth of the space. Objects of the same size are shown smaller the further away they are.
2. The principle of <u>staggering</u> is that any object behind another is hidden. Care should be taken that the lines do not overlap, as if they do they cannot be interpreted in spatial terms.
3. The principal of <u>correct level of detail</u> can be compared with architects' plans, which use different scales. Objects in the foreground are close and are therefore depicted in detail; objects that are closer to the horizon are further away and therefore some of the precise detail is lost. Here the draughtsman or woman varies the degree of abstraction.
4. Someone who has a good long-distance view in the city or the country recognises that the layers of air and vapour cause tonal values to fade or grow weaker towards the horizon. This is the <u>atmospheric principle</u>. The same object, seen at a greater distance, tends to blur visually in the background.
5. The fifth principle of perspective drawing deals with <u>shadows</u>, which with all their different facets can create strong spatial effects.

The way the picture is built up is an important decision that must be made before starting every drawing, and may decide on the success or failure of the work. A drawing is always only a depicted part of the surroundings. There are complicated ways of showing the whole of these

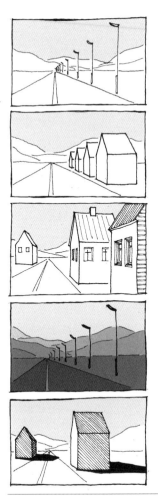

Fig. 72: The five principles of perspective
illustration: spatial constant, staggering,
correct level of detail, atmosphere,
shadows

surroundings in perspective, but essentially a part or section must be
chosen – consciously or unconsciously. First of all, the picture plane must
be determined, that is, you must decide what you want to draw. The imaginary picture plane (PP) lies between you and the object you draw.
> Fig. 73 It is like an invisible plane slid between draughtsperson and sub-
ject, and projects what the observer sees onto the drawing sheet at a
reduced scale.

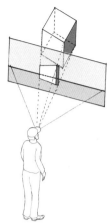

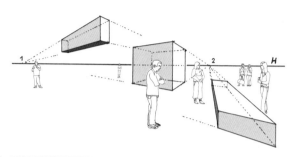

Fig. 73: Between architecture and draughts-man lies the picture plane: the drawing sheet.

Fig. 74: Three-dimensional volumes in relation to the position of the horizon

Before starting the drawing you must discover your relationship to the subject of the drawing. Is it above or below you? Where is the horizon? How many vanishing points are there? The horizon (H) is always at our eye level, whether we are lying on the ground (frog perspective), sitting or standing. If all the people gathered on a level square were of the same size, then their eyes would all be at the same height and therefore directed towards the line of the horizon. > Fig. 74 Depending on interest the subject of the (draughtsperson's) desire is either above the horizon (H), at the same height as the horizon or below it. Vanishing points (VP) always lie on the horizon line (except for tilted planes and three point perspectives).

The station point from which a building is viewed influences the kind of perspective (central, two-point or three-point perspective). If you look at a building or an interior space at right angles, you must draw the perspective with a single vanishing point (central perspective). The special aspect of the central perspective is that only the lines of building edges that are parallel and run in space converge at the central vanishing point; all the other lines have no vanishing point and therefore never meet. If you are not looking at the building at right angles but at an outside corner of the building, you have a diagonal or two-point perspective. Left-hand building parts converge towards a left hand vanishing point, right hand building parts towards the right-hand point. As the name suggests, the two-point perspective has two vanishing points. All the vertical edges of the rectangular volume remain vertical. If we draw an angled view and at the same time look upwards, for instance at the base of a high-rise) or

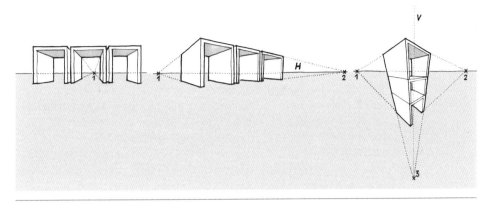

Fig. 75: System of the central perspective, two-point perspective, and three-point perspective

look downwards, (for instance out of the window of a high-rise building), a third vanishing point is added. This is then – with a rectangular building – the three-point perspective. Theoretically we could draw a spherical perspective that depicts the space surrounding us in all directions. In a rectilinear world one would always have six vanishing points, four them every 90° in the four points of the compass and one each for the high point and the low point. The high point and low point lie on what is called the "vertizon" (V), the equivalent of the horizon.   ■ ●

■ **Tip:** Essentially, the nearer you are to the building you are drawing, the closer together the vanishing points are on the drawing sheet (see Fig. 63, page 59). If you move further away from the building and draw it again you will notice that in relation the vanishing points are now further away from the building, possibly even no longer on the drawing sheet. In single point perspectives the vanishing point is generally near the centre of the sheet.

● **Important:** A significant difference from the technical architectural drawing is the depiction only of what is visible, i.e. no edges of volumes that lie behind or in front of the building being drawn are indicated by dashed or dotted lines. Unless, that is, various lines are needed to construct building parts: lines to discover the horizon, vanishing points or construction lines for complicated building parts can be retained in the finished drawing, as they form part of the development and comprehension process of the drawing. Corrections are also allowed. The aim is to find the correct line and to depict the subject of the drawing correctly.

Construction of an on-site perspective

The perspective most commonly used in on-site drawing is the diagonal or two-point perspective with two vanishing points. The individual steps of the construction are described below.

If, with your arm outstretched, you hold the pen or pencil horizontally in front of your eyes and imagine the line produced, you obtain the position of the horizon. This can be transferred to the sheet as a straight horizontal line. In the present situation this can be done on the lower part of the sheet, as at the moment the level of your eyes (approx. 1.50 m above the level of the ground) is in the lower part of the building. Now you can see what is to be drawn above and below the horizon. With a two-point perspective it is advisable to draw the building edge closest to the point where you are standing as a vertical. > Fig. 76

Finding the vanishing points is most important. First of all, the actual length of the building edge is drawn on the verticals. This also determines the size of the drawing. The pencil is an ideal instrument for measuring the lengths, angles and proportions. It can be placed directly against the lines of streets, building edges, or sloping roofs. If you measure the angles of the lines running from the end points of the building edges and continue these lines to the horizon you obtain the two vanishing points. The width and height of the building you are looking at can be measured with the pencil: fix your thumb at a certain point on the pencil and read this length in relation to the entire length of the pencil. > Fig. 77

Taking further measurements completes the volume of the building in all directions. The position of the projecting pediment can be determined by drawing two diagonals through the rectangular area. The main
■ openings of the building are also drawn. > Fig. 78

■ **Tip:** To arrive at comparable results you should always hold your arm outstretched against the subject of the drawing, no matter what you wish to measure. In measuring angles a watch face can also be helpful. A sloping roof must not always be described by a number of degrees, the detail "two o'clock" can also suffice.

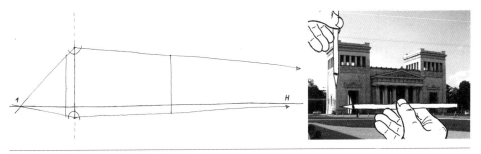

Fig. 76: Determining the position of the horizon and a near building corner with the drawing pen or pencil

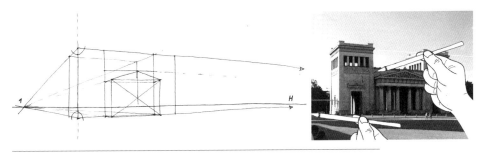

Fig. 77: Finding the vanishing points and measuring the building's height and width

Now the drawing can be completed. Secondary openings, ornament and details are added. The <u>foreground</u> and <u>background</u> frame the building. Applying shadows gives the architectural drawing a certain plasticity. > Fig. 79

In the simpler central perspective first of all look you for the point on the end face (for instance of the building) that is exactly at right angles to the station point. This point lies on the horizon. From the corner points of the end face of the building – or perhaps an opening or an imaginary surface – lines are drawn from the direction of the vanishing point.
> Figs. 90 and 91, page 87

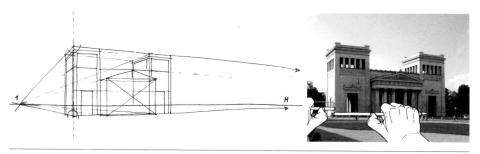

Fig. 78: Completing the volume by measuring

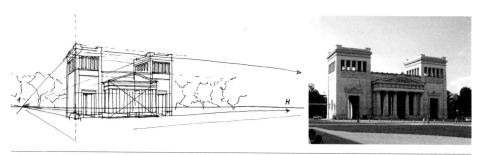

Fig. 79: Completing the drawing

Site plan and floor plan

If you wish to have an overview of the place where the building stands a small site plan sketch is ideal. The site plan is essential for depicting the urban setting. You can attempt to survey the space with the help of the perspective but walking across it is also extremely useful. Walk around the building, which is ideally freestanding, taking paces of equal length. To make an approximately correct site plan, it is useful first of all to draw a chequerboard <u>grid</u> on the sheet. Then – depending on the size of the place – the width and length of each square represents ten to twenty paces. You should now walk across the area and attempt to insert the building at the right position in this grid. You can also do it at a smaller scale by just looking at the building and drawing its outline rather than a site plan. Here you walk around the outsides of a freestanding building and count your paces. This helps you discover the outline or footprint, i.e. the relationship of width to length. If it is possible to get inside the building you wish to draw, you can continue drawing the floor plan in the interior and in this way depict the building's function.

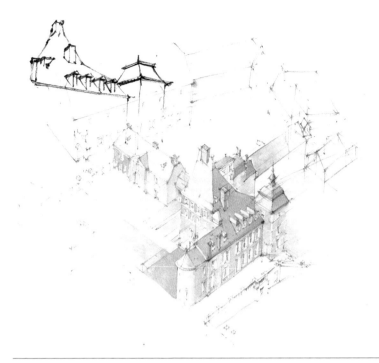

Fig. 80: Axonometric projection made on site

Floor plan axonometric

If the outline of the floor plan has been drawn you can attempt a further type of architectural drawing, the axonometric depiction. This is, alongside the perspective, the drawing that is best able to provide information about the configuration of the building volume. On the basis of the plan drawing (generally immediately above or below it) using extended <u>construction lines</u>, make an attempt to depict the building in three dimensions. Walls and columns, for example, are given certain heights. Through further observations, as the result of walking around and inside the building several times, you can then complete the drawing.

Elevation and section

If you wish to convey the special proportions of the building on site the elevation drawing is recommended. Alongside the perspective this is most useful drawing for depicting the proportions of a building. You can achieve command of the correct degree of abstraction at different scales (i.e. drawing sizes) by producing several elevations, each time at a different distance from the building. You should attempt to ignore the marginal central perspective offered by your view of the building. With access to the building, you can sketch a cross section based on the elevation, which shows the structural system of the building or its circulation system.

AIDS
Grid and frame

With a transparent grid of lines or a mesh, which can easily be made on a sheet of film, you can recognise several important aspects. If, like most sheets of drawing paper, the sheet of film is roughly in the format 2:3 it can be used as a basis for positioning a drawing on the sheet, by holding it at the desired distance away from yourself and looking at the building through the transparent film. If you hold one of the horizontal lines directly in front of your eyes you also obtain the horizon. You also see all the building verticals, which for a one- or two-point perspective, are always drawn as verticals. The transparent grid provides further aid if you have difficulty in transferring the correct <u>proportions</u> of the building and its surroundings to the sheet of paper. The structure of the gridded sheet of film can be applied lightly to the sheet with the drawing. You now examine the "contents" of each square and draw these, square by square, onto the sheet. Gradually the sheet is filled with the correct proportions.

A frame, which can also be made with the thumb and index finger of both hands, can help to find the section or part of the reality in front of you that you wish to draw. It gives you a feeling for what you can fit on the sheet, and helps avoid unpleasant surprises with regard to the size of drawing. The area of the frame always represents the drawing sheet.

Preliminary sketch

Before making a larger perspective drawing it is sometimes advisable first of all to draw a small preliminary sketch of what you plan to do. This should help deal with problems as regards the relationship in which you stand to the building, where the horizon is, and how many vanishing points there are and whether they are on the <u>drawing sheet</u> at all. It should give you a feeling for how the drawing can be positioned on the sheet. The frame of the preliminary drawing represents the outer edges of the drawing sheet. The horizon is quickly found and entered in the lower third of the sheet, then by measuring the angles the two essential vanishing points can be found. The rough outline of the building can now be added faintly. The quick note represented by the preliminary drawing trains your ability to grasp and perceive, both of which are essential for drawing on site. The <u>miniature drawing</u> also helps to decide how large to make the drawing that follows the preliminary one.

Fig. 81: Using a sheet of film with a grid of lines that divides up the building, which is distorted in perspective, into areas of equal size

Fig. 82: Use of the frame

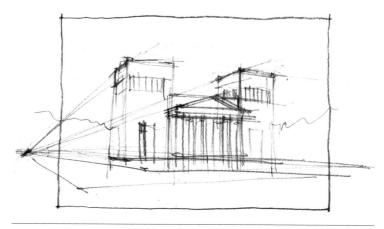

Fig. 83: Miniature preliminary drawing based on the content of the frame (here a two-point perspective, station point in the lower part of the building)

Construction aids

In diagonal perspectives the sides of buildings are often so distorted that you cannot grasp the visual centre point of the building without being irritated by this distortion. To determine where the visual centre point of a building seen in perspective lies, take the pencil with your thumb at the centre of its length and hold it in front of your eyes. Now move the pencil towards or away from you until the length of the pencil exactly covers the building that you want to draw. If you look again at your thumb and note the point of the building that is hidden behind it, you obtain the centre point of the building and of the drawing you are about to make and can position it better on the sheet.

For instance, in order to depict regularly spaced street lamps in perspective you must first of all choose a distance (D) between two street lamps. Then you determine the middle line (M) of the two lamps and connect this with the vanishing point (VP). From the top of the first lamp you now draw a diagonal through the middle point of the second lamp and extend it to meet a bottom point on the lower vanishing line. This is the point at which the third lamp stands.

You find the middle point of vertical lines in a perspective by measuring the actual length or height of the lines. In contrast, the middle point (M) of rectangular areas is found by drawing an "X" through a rectangular area in perspective. Centrally positioned building elements (flags, towers, windows) can then be more easily constructed from this middle point.

Fig. 84: Finding the visual focus of the building

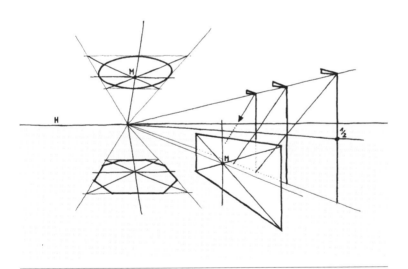

Fig. 85: Construction aids

Circles are always found within squares, ellipses within a rectangle. From the square or rectangle with an "X" drawn through it we arrive at the circle or the ellipse through the intermediate step of the octagon.

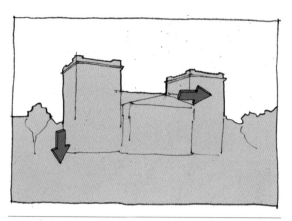

Fig. 86: Approach to drawing with outlines (see also Fig. 73, page 72)

Outlines

Drawing a perspective correctly is often difficult. There are, however, a number of approaches to depicting the object correctly. In drawing outlines or intermediate spaces first of all the contour is depicted that separates, say, the stone building from the airy sky or defines the void/space between two volumes. On this basis the relationships between two volumes are first determined, not the volumes themselves. Once the main outline, which can be drawn intuitively or by measuring, is established on the sheet the building can be completed below the outline. While making the outline compare the lengths, angles and relationships just drawn with those you drew just a short time earlier. The outline is thus a scale for itself and later has a considerable influence on the composition of the drawing as a whole.

Shadows

Light makes buildings, objects and people visible but it is shadows that make them seem alive in reality. If you are able to identify and depict shadows a drawing becomes more spatial and has greater relief. There are different ways of transferring this spatiality to the two-dimensional drawing substrate. The path of the sun should be noted and followed while making a drawing, as in the course of producing an elaborate drawing it can change (and along with it the shadows). When the sun shines different kinds of shadows can be identified on buildings. The side facing towards the light of a rectangular building is brighter than the side of the building opposite. The sides of the building between them are,

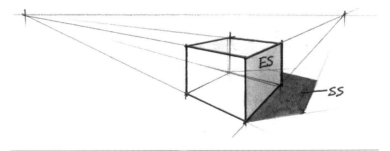

Fig. 87: An object's own shadow and cast shadow (light source on the left)

in terms of brightness, somewhere in between. A distinction is drawn between <u>own shadow</u> and <u>cast shadow</u>. Own shadow (OS) is, as a rule, lighter than cast shadow (CS). If own shadow and cast shadow meet they produce what is called core shadow. Pure shadow drawings have a special kind of attractiveness. Here the focus is on depicting the different <u>tonal values</u> of the shadows. Medium light tones are avoided and particularly light and dark areas are exaggerated. The brightest surface remains white. If the drawing is made on grey or brown paper the brightest area can also be made using a white pencil, which achieves a similar effect.

> Fig. 10, page 18

Instruments for when you are on the move

You should feel at ease with your own drawing instruments or utensils. They should be agreeable to use and, for daily use, they should all fit easily into a bag. The equipment needed for drawing in the city need not be elaborate; it must only suffice for what you intend to do.

A fisherman's seat, a stool or even a <u>draughtsman's stool</u> are recommended to every urban draughtsman or woman. If you do not have a stool you have to find a position where you can sit comfortably for a length of time, but which then may not offer the view you want. During the colder part of the year, fingerless <u>gloves</u>, which allow you to hold the pencil properly, are very useful. What are known as fold-back <u>clips</u> are handy to prevent the wind whipping up the pages while you are drawing on site. Drawings made with a lot of graphite or charcoal should be treated with a

Fig. 88: The draughtsperson's utensils

fixative to ensure a long life. If you do not have this protective layer (generally available in spray cans) with you, a temporary solution is to lay a
■ ○ loose empty sheet over your drawing.

■ **Tip:** Drawing architecture on site marked by external influences: a strong wind, hot sun, bright backlight, annoying pigeons and inquisitive passers-by or unpleasant smells, the public realm that cannot be influenced, atmospheric morning light or a spontaneous feeling for a particular piece of architecture. Drawing buildings on site also means observing rules. You should be certain that it is permitted to draw at the chosen spot. It is indeed often the case that drawing is allowed where photography is forbidden, but where this is uncertain you should make enquiries.

○ **Note:** In public space, your choice of drawing subjects may place you at prominent and busy places and squares. You should not let yourself be discouraged by the comments of passers-by. If you feel watched by an audience behind you, you should close your sketchbook briefly until the inquisitive glances have turned elsewhere. You do not need to put up with this kind of thing: after all, the author of the drawing is the only relevant person, not the public at large. You should observe the influences and rules, particularly if the drawing takes a longer period of time.

Further development

AS-BUILT DRAWING

Design sketching can also be combined with drawing architecture on site. For instance, where you intend to prepare a design for an empty inner city site, you should first of all visit the site. With the sketchbook all the relevant data and impressions of the site can be noted and the spatial situation recorded in a drawing. After this urban design analysis a perspective of the empty site, without the future design, can be made directly. You should look for a perspective that shows the main characteristics of the site.

When the design has matured in terms of function and form it can be integrated into the drawing made on site using sketching paper or tracing paper. The planned volume, which previously existed only in the form of planar projections, can now be evaluated in spatial and urban planning terms. Care should be taken to insert the design correctly into the drawing in terms of perspective, taking into account the horizon and vanishing point(s).

Naturally, this can also be done on the basis of a photograph of the site or even of the model of the surroundings. First of all, however, the horizon and vanishing points must be determined, which can be drawn using sketching paper.

DIGITALISATION AND IMAGE EDITING

Freehand drawings are always <u>originals</u>, of which only one exists. In some cases, however, digital reproductions are needed, whether for screen presentations, presentation drawings or website contents. The digitalisation of a drawing is almost always followed by editing the image on the computer, no matter whether the drawing was pixelated by a scanner or a camera. This is true of both design drawings and on-site drawings.

Digitalisation

If sketches or architectural drawings are required in digital form for a particular purpose, there are essentially two ways in which this can be done.

Scanning drawings with a <u>flatbed image scanner</u> is a very good and authentic solution. The scanner has image processing software that allows the settings to be adjusted. The resolution should be 300 dpi, which is high, but still acceptable in terms of data volume. The drawing is laid flat and evenly on the scanner. As a result the distance of the drawing to

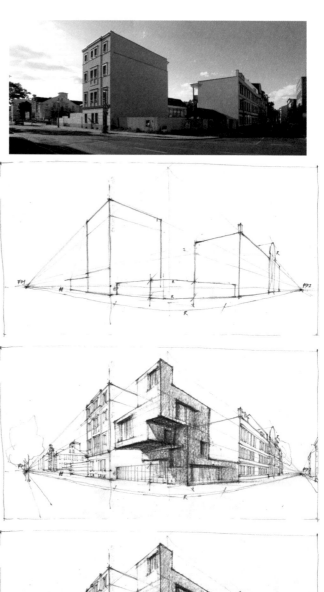

Fig. 89: Photograph of the empty site, construction of the perspective, insertion of the design volume, developing the image, completing the illustration

Fig 90: Scanning vs. photographing a drawing

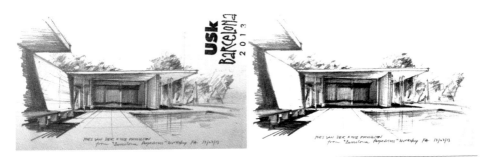

Fig. 91: Drawing before and after cleaning

the light source remains the same, allowing you to expect a homogenous result. If only a DIN A4 scanner is available, larger documents can be scanned in sections and later pieced together with the image editing program in the panorama or sorting function. Care should be taken that the individual data are always scanned and saved in the same way.

Drawings can also be <u>photographed</u>. If you want to do this indoors you should ensure even, ideally indirect, lighting so that no reflections impair the depiction of the drawing. Reflections occur in particular with pencil drawings and drawings made on tracing paper. The photograph must be taken perpendicular to the drawing so that it is not distorted. The photographer's shadow should not be cast. The direct flash function of the camera should always be deactivated. If you attempt to make a photographic reproduction outdoors, in principle the same rules apply: no reflections, no shadows, and even lighting. In this way, both with an overcast sky and in bright sunshine, good results can be achieved.

Postprocessing a design drawing

After the drawing has been digitalised, image editing is usually necessary to allow the drawing to be used for other purposes. For instance, after a drawing on sketching paper has been scanned or photographed, grey areas and edges caused by unevenness may often impair the image. Bleeding may be evident directly beside lines, or the original grey or black of the lines may not be recognisable.

With a purely line drawing for which only pencil or fineliner was used it makes sense to reduce the saturation level of the entire image so that it still has a number of different shades of grey (caution: do not active "greyscale" editing as this changes the compatibility of the file). If the drawing now looks rather pale, correcting the gradation curve can help. Using the white pipette (black pipette) a white (black) area is marked in the drawing. In this way all blurred grey areas in the drawing can be removed, and the individual lines now appear more clearly. Changes to image brightness and contrast produce similar results.

Having been cleaned up the drawing offers a good basis for further editing and processing with areas of colour, colour gradients and transparencies. A collage-like mounting of people, trees and other indicators of scale in a hand drawing can achieve a delightful effect. Here, it is important that the additional elements be allocated to a separate layer in the image editing program so that later changes can be made. > Fig. 89 below

Postprocessing an on-site drawing

An architectural drawing that was made on site can also be subsequently edited, for instance on the basis of a photograph. Care should be taken that the place remains authentic and is not falsified by incorrectly cast shadows, exaggerated colours, or changes to the depictions of material.

In Fig. 92 right, the background was first completely covered with a mid-grey and then the lightest areas (the windows and the soffit of the arch) created by removing this colour. Special effects here include the angled entry of light, created by means of a white transparent surface, and the reflections on the floor, transparent duplicates, turned upside down, of the respective original layers in the image editing program. Fig. 93 underlines the horizontality of the design by the atmospheric addition of sky and vegetation as a gradient and through the emphasis of the horizon. Here, too, the depicting the shadows correctly is most important.

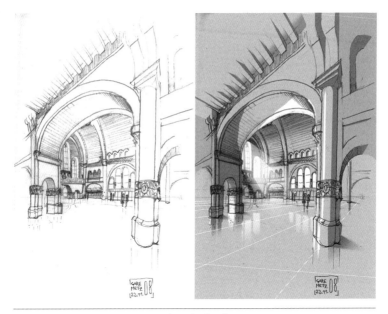

Fig. 92: Original and digitally processed on-site drawing

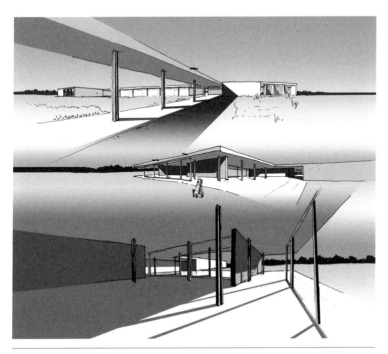

Fig. 93: Digital processing of on-site drawings

In conclusion

Drawing is the architect's language. The technical drawing is not as personally formulated as the freehand sketch but is tied to certain conventions. When such a drawing is made by hand the placing of focal points and particular care can create an individual style. However, the use of CAD programs in the early design stages makes drawing styles more uniform and interchangeable and increasingly reduces the proportion of freely drawn ideas in a design. Even while still a student the growing complexity of the tasks that confront the architect reduces the use of the freehand drawing, which is often seen as excessively time-consuming.

But it is precisely the spontaneous and intuitive freehand drawing that can transfer the ideas of the designer to a sheet of paper in a pure manner. Here, sketching is learnt by trial and error. To be able to use this medium in a confident and effective way, certain techniques and tools must be tried out. In the later stage of the design it forms a perfect synthesis with model building and technical drawing.

Sketching architecture on site provides a valuable service. It offers the draughtsman or woman a very personal abstraction of what has been perceived. The archive of architectural structures and quotations that is gradually built up through drawing existing architecture can be later drawn upon when designing. But here, too, drawing architecture cannot claim to replace other disciplines of architectural education. Visiting a building in its setting in urban space or in the landscape, going inside it, touching it and discovering its various functional, constructive or design characteristics are also an essential part of perceiving and understanding a building.

Appendix

LITERATURE

Jonathan Andrews: *Architectural Visions. Contemporary Sketches, Perspectives, Drawings,* Braun, Salenstein 2010

Alejandro Bahamón: *Sketch: Houses,* Loft Publications, Barcelona 2008

Herman van Bergeijk and Deborah Hauptmann: *Notations of Herman Hertzberger,* Nai Publishers, Rotterdam 1998

Bert Bielefeld (ed.): *Basics Architectural Presentation,* Birkhäuser Verlag, Basel 2014

Matthew Brehm: *Sketching on location,* Kendall Hut Publishing Company, Dubuque 2012

Gabriel Campanario: *The Art of Urban Sketching,* Quarry Books, Beverly 2012

Francis D. K. Ching: *Architecture: Form, Space & Order,* John Wiley & Sons, Hoboken 2007, 3rd edition

Magali Delgado Yanes and Ernest Redondo Dominguez: *Freehand Drawing for Architects and Interior Designers,* Parramon Paidotribo, Barcelona 2005

Brian Edwards: *Understanding Architecture Through Drawing,* E & FN Spon, London 1994

Helmut Germer and Thomas Neeser: *1D The First Dimension: Drawing and Perception – A Workbook for Designers,* Birkhäuser, Basel 2010

Danny Gregory: *An illustrated life. Drawing inspiration from the private sketchbooks of artists, illustrators and designers,* How Books, Cincinnati 2008

Eric Jenkins: *Drawn to Design. Analyzing Architecture Through Freehand Drawing,* Birkhäuser, Basel 2013

Cathy Johnson: *Artist's Journal Workshop. Creating your life in words and pictures,* F&W Media, Newton Abbot 2011

Natascha Meuser: *Construction and Design Manual. Architectural Drawings,* DOM publishers, Berlin 2012

Grant W. Reid: *Landscape Graphics. Plan, Section, and Perspective Drawing of Landscape Spaces,* Watson-Guptill Publications, New York 2002

James Richards: *Freehand Drawing and Discovery: Urban Sketching and Concept Drawing for Designers,* John Wiley & Sons, Hoboken 2013

Francesca Serrazanetti and Matteo Schubert: *La mano dell'architetto. The hand of the architect,* FAI – Fondo Ambiente Italiano/Moleskine srl/Editrice Abitare Segesta, Milan 2009

PICTURE CREDITS

THE AUTHOR

Florian Afflerbach, Dipl.-Ing. (FH) Architekt M. A., is a research assistant at the Chair for Spatial Design at Siegen University and the Chair for the Depiction of Architecture at the TU Dortmund. He is a co-founder of Schaff-Verlag für Architekturvermittlung, Hamburg.

Basics Roof Construction
Tanja Brotrück
ISBN 978-3-7643-7683-3

Basics Timber Construction
Ludwig Steiger
ISBN 978-3-7643-8102-8

Available as a compendium:
Basics Building Construction
Bert Bielefeld (ed.)
ISBN 978-3-0356-0372-9

Professional Practice
Basics Tendering
Tim Brandt,
Sebastian Franssen
ISBN 978-3-7643-8110-3

Basics Project Planning
Hartmut Klein
ISBN 978-3-7643-8469-2

Basics Site Management
Lars-Phillip Rusch
ISBN 978-3-7643-8104-2

Basics Time Management
Bert Bielefeld
ISBN 978-3-7643-8873-7

Basics Budgeting
Bert Bielefeld, Roland Schneider
ISBN 978-3-03821-532-5

Available as a compendium:
Basics Project Management
Architecture
Bert Bielefeld (ed.)
ISBN 978-3-03821-462-5

Urbanism
Basics Urban Building Blocks
Thorsten Bürklin,
Michael Peterek
ISBN 978-3-7643-8460-9

Basics Urban Analysis
Gerrit Schwalbach
ISBN 978-3-7643-8938-3

**Building Physics/
Building Services**
Basics Room Conditioning
Oliver Klein, Jörg Schlenger
ISBN 978-3-7643-8664-1

Basics Water Cycles
Doris Haas-Arndt
ISBN 978-3-7643-8854-6

Landscape Architecture
Basics Designing with Plants
Regine Ellen Wöhrle,
Hans-Jörg Wöhrle
ISBN 978-3-7643-8659-7

Basics Designing with Water
Axel Lohrer, Cornelia Bott
ISBN 978-3-7643-8662-7

www.birkhauser.com

Series editor: Bert Bielefeld
Concept: Bert Bielefeld, Annette Gref

Translation from German into English:
James Roderick O'Donovan
English copy editing: Monica Buckland
Project management: Petra Schmid
Layout, cover design and typography:
Andreas Hidber
Typesetting and production: Amelie Solbrig

Library of Congress Cataloging-in-Publication
data
A CIP catalog record for this book has been
applied for at the Library of Congress.

Bibliographic information published by the
German National Library
The German National Library lists this publica-
tion in the Deutsche Nationalbibliografie;
detailed bibliographic data are available on
the Internet at http://dnb.dnb.de.

This book is also available in a German language
edition (ISBN 978-3-03821-543-1).

© 2014 Birkhäuser Verlag GmbH, Basel
P.O. Box 44, 4009 Basel, Switzerland
Part of Walter de Gruyter GmbH, Berlin/Boston

Printed on acid-free paper produced from
chlorine-free pulp. TCF ∞

Printed in Germany

ISBN 978-3-03821-545-5

9 8 7 6 5 4 3 2

www.birkhauser.com